KILLING LIONS

KILLING LIONS

A GUIDE THROUGH THE TRIALS YOUNG MEN FACE

JOHN ELDREDGE
& SAM ELDREDGE

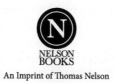

NELSON
BOOKS

An Imprint of Thomas Nelson

Published in Nashville, Tennessee, by Nelson Books, an imprint of Thomas Nelson. Nelson Books and Thomas Nelson are registered trademarks of HarperCollins Christian Publishing, Inc.

The authors are represented by Yates and Yates, LLP, 1100 Town & Country Road, Suite 1300, Orange, California 92868. Thomas Nelson, Inc., titles may be purchased in bulk for educational, business, fund-raising, or sales promotional use. For information, please e-mail SpecialMarkets@ThomasNelson.com.

Unless otherwise noted, Scripture quotations are taken from the Holy Bible, New International Version®, NIV®. Copyright © 1973, 1978, 1984, 2011 by Biblica, Inc.™ Used by permission of Zondervan. All rights reserved worldwide. www.zondervan.com

Scripture quotations marked MSG are taken from *The Message* by Eugene H. Peterson. © 1993, 1994, 1995, 1996, 2000. Used by permission of NavPress Publishing Group. All rights reserved.

The names and identifying characteristics of some individuals have been changed to protect their privacy.

ISBN: 978-0-529-11691-8 (IE)

Cataloging-in-Publication Data available through the Library of Congress
ISBN: 978-1-4002-0670-4

Printed in the United States of America
14 15 16 17 18 RRD 6 5 4 3 2 1

To Susie, for believing in me before I did.
—Sam

*To Sam, Blaine, and Luke, who have cut a
path for the young men traveling with them and
coming hard after them. You are the real deal.*
—Dad

*And to the young men whose lives have
helped to shape this book, and to the young
men whose lives this book will shape.*
—John and Sam

Contents

Add to this that he was partly a young man of our time—that is, honest by nature, demanding the truth, seeking it and believing in it, and in that belief demanding immediate participation in it with all the strength of his soul; demanding an immediate deed, with an unfailing desire to sacrifice everything for this deed, even life. Although, unfortunately, these young men do not understand that the sacrifice of life is, perhaps, the easiest of all sacrifices in many cases, while to sacrifice, for example, five or six years of their ebulliently youthful life to hard, difficult studies, to learning, in order to increase tenfold their strength to serve the very truth and the very deed that they loved and set out to accomplish—such sacrifice is quite often almost beyond the strength of many of them.

—Fyodor Dostoevsky,
The Brothers Karamazov

Preface

In the summer of 2012 I found myself one year out of college and suddenly facing a host of questions. When I left the mountains of Colorado for the beaches of California to pursue a college education, I did it without much forethought. I liked the warmer weather, the campus was beautiful, and I needed to get out from under the guy I had been in my parents' home. Most of my decisions in those years were made impulsively. *Do I like what it has to offer? Okay, I'll do it.*

Then I graduated. After the first few months of elation that freedom and being on your own can bring, I found myself floundering. I had jumped into the deep end of the pool that is life in your twenties, and it felt like I was treading water and getting nowhere. Life was getting more complicated by the week, and my ability to choose the right direction for myself was falling apart. Truth is, I was taking on water.

Like most of the young men I know, I want to be self-sufficient. I want to struggle for my own direction and step out in pursuit of my dreams. I want to know it all and never ask for help. This is how most of the guys I know approach young manhood—on their own, never asking for help, wandering through these years, and pretending they are doing better than they really are.

Maybe my fuel ran out faster. Maybe I knew I didn't have to go it alone if I didn't want to. Whatever the reason, I stopped one day and asked my dad if we could talk about how things were going for me. What followed were weekly phone calls where we would dive in to my struggles and seek answers together—conversations not all men get but, I think, all of us desperately want. This book is a result of those conversations, an opportunity for us to flesh out the process for your benefit.

The story ebbs and flows in and out of the college years, searching for meaningful work, pursuing a young woman, getting married, and chasing my dreams. None of this is fabricated—the questions are real, the doubts are real, the answers are real. The interaction between father and son is real.

I recently read an article about a young Maasai man who came to the United States to pursue his master's degree and then a doctoral degree. Before arriving in the Western world, the young warrior had killed a lion in order to protect his village and their cattle. This practice is deep in their tradition—that young men must face and defeat a lion with a spear, should it attack their livestock. He had been badly wounded, as one would expect, but after slaying the predator he was regarded as a hero and a leader. I can't imagine any university final or job interview being very daunting for a man with lion scars across his chest.

There was something about that story that spoke to the deep places in my soul—something about having faced a great challenge, one in which victory was far from certain, yet conquering it, that makes me wonder. If I had prevailed through my own great trial, would I walk taller or carry a greater confidence into this uncertain future? I can't help but think: if I had taken down a lion, life wouldn't feel like I'm heading out into the bush with only an iPhone at my side.

And so we offer this book as a confession, an invitation, and a manifesto for a generation.

It is my confession, because I hope that in telling my story you might find you are asking the same questions. It is our invitation to journey with us, to be the son who receives fathering or to be the father who learns what must be spoken to his son. It is a manifesto for the generation that is rising up and knows not how to begin the lion hunt or what face our lions are hiding behind. We believe that with a little help you can be the man you long to be—the man the world needs you to be.

Sam Eldredge
Minneapolis, Minnesota

one

College and Then What?

As he mused about these things, he realized that he had to choose between thinking of himself as the poor victim of a thief and as an adventurer in quest of his treasure. "I'm an adventurer, looking for treasure," he said to himself.

—Paulo Coelho, *The Alchemist*

I don't think I told you just how pathetic my first job was. Probably because I was embarrassed.

I was twenty-two years old, the ink still wet on my college diploma—from a prestigious West Coast school, I might add—and I had joined the workforce as a professional . . . errand runner. Some large companies employ people in positions known as rabbits. (Somehow I get the feeling these folks forgo the business cards.) I found my job on Craigslist under the title "Runner" and thought to myself, *I go running.*

It's not that my job was particularly demanding; in fact it was the mind-numbing triviality that I found so disheartening. To give you an example of an average day's list for the (very) wealthy family that signed the checks:

- one case Diet Coke
- three cases lime Perrier
- twelve single-serving AvoDerm cat food (No prawn or liver flavor. Their cat, Taco, has already sent me back to return said flavors on multiple occasions. And who names their cat Taco, anyway?)
- two gallons distilled water
- plain Greek yogurt
- Milton's crackers
- lunch for the staff of eighteen from a local hot spot (After triple checking that Angie's salad has sunflower seeds and that Lynn's custom smoothie is accounted for; all dressing on the side.)
- drop packages off at UPS, and a case of wine at a fellow board member's house in town

I felt like a joke. First jobs are infamous; everyone complains about them just like an angst-filled teenager would. But as I drove around town, flipping from station to station on the radio for what seemed like hours that would not end, I couldn't help but wonder, *What am I doing with my life?* My friends who took the business track landed jobs working for music advertising agencies and accounting firms; one was working for a tech start-up. A fellow English graduate manned the front desk of a fancy hotel so Paris Hilton could pursue her hobby of DJ-ing. But when we gathered around the table at Dargan's on Friday evenings, I wasn't so sure the "business savvy" majors were really doing any better than me. They were disappointed too.

The weekends raced by, and I would return every Monday to my mind-numbing job so I could pay for food and rent, so I could go back to work, in order to pay for more food and rent. It felt so cyclical, the never-ending water-tread test to graduate into the adult pool.

Maybe this story should start in my sophomore year of college, back when the birds were chirping, the sun shone every day, and everyone laughed so easily. Back when we had to declare our majors. The decision felt like career day all over again—each student choosing what he wanted to be when he grew up. I chose English because I love stories and creativity, and I want to be a writer. I still can't stand the reaction when I tell people what my major is: "*Oh*"—always in the tone of someone hearing bad news—"What are you going to do with *that*?" I want to shoot back, "How does 'not sit in a cubicle for the rest of my life' sound, you sellout?" But now, two years later, it isn't so easy to convince myself I made the right decision after all. I wonder, *Did I totally waste my time in college? Dad?*

The MBA who bussed my table last night and the bachelor of architecture who helped me find something at Barnes & Noble are wondering the same thing. And so the great battle begins in earnest: the battle for your heart, the battle to find a life worth living, the battle not to *lose* heart as you find a life worth living.

So take a deep breath, and step back from the ledge. Every move into the unknown usually feels like free-falling at first. I remember those feelings myself. College is a staging ground. But for what? To think clearly about the college years, ask yourself, are you simply a laborer, a careerist in an endless economic cycle? Or are you a human being, and that heart beating deep within you is telling you of a life of purpose and meaning you were created to live? You see, Sam, the questions of who we *are* and why we are here are far more important questions than how to land a great job and make money. You don't want to fall into a life you end up hating. Years ago I was counseling a successful dentist in his late forties—listening to his confession, really. He was doing well, lived in a nice house, took exciting vacations—and was thoroughly depressed. After a long pause he lamented, "I had no idea what I wanted when I was in college; I was someone else when I chose this life."

The idea that eighteen-year-olds have some grasp on who they are and what they ought to do for the rest of their lives is madness. A college freshman has barely begun to think about his life or separate himself from his family and culture enough to see the world clearly. Waking up in time for class is an accomplishment; remembering to do laundry a personal triumph.

My first year in college felt like camp. Everybody was so giddy to be there, so wrapped up in the excitement and freedom of it all, that it hardly felt like school half the time. We would blow off assignments, head to the beach, stay up late playing Mafia or beer pong, and flirt with everyone. Some took up smoking, others serial dating, and the only thing we could think of was the fact that we were free. Free from our hometowns and our parents' rules. Free from who and what we had been in high school. Plenty of time ahead of us to figure it all out. It was its own reality.

Which is fine—freshmen are freshmen. But you don't ask those campers to define their life course, for heaven's sake. They've got a world of discovery and a few rude awakenings ahead, all of which must come first. This is a season for exploration and transformation—discovering both who we are and what we love, what our place in the world might be. Our dreams and desires need to awaken, grow, and mature. *We* need to awaken, grow, and mature so that we might be able to handle those desires and dreams. The man I was becoming at eighteen was far from the man I had become by thirty and leagues from who I am today at fifty-three. There's no shame in that; this is how life works, for everyone. Who came up with the notion that the day you graduate from college you are a fully developed adult stepping into a wonderful and fully developed life? It's about as crazy as it is frustrating.

And it's a lie. I think you'd be better served if you picture this season as a journey through a wild country filled with beauty and danger—and a few swamps—than expecting it to be a clear and defined road of College-Work-Life-Done.

There are two basic approaches to college education. Plan A is merely "career grooming." Choose the professional trajectory your life will take, follow the prescribed courses that will prepare you to enter that profession, and proceed as quickly as possible up the ranks. I understand the appeal of this approach because it seems to make sense and promise results—at least on paper. Colleges love to promise career results, and parents love those promises. But there are an awful lot of disappointed econ majors out there working at Starbucks. "Follow this plan and you'll get this life" can be a real shocker when it doesn't pan out; it leaves you feeling betrayed if this was the assumption you were working under. This is especially true in a volatile global economy.

Plan A ignores one vital piece of reality: very few people end up working in the field they studied in college. I don't know anyone, personally. Even my doctor friend grew tired of the medical profession and now works in a nonprofit. I majored in theater as an undergrad and then did a master's in counseling; Mom chose sociology. Now we are both writers. Life just doesn't follow a clean, clear, and linear path. More importantly, *people* don't.

I'm reading a fascinating book called *Shop Class as Soulcraft*; the author is a young man who graduated with a doctorate in political philosophy from the University of Chicago, took a sweet job as executive director of a Washington think tank, found himself constantly tired and dispirited, and after six months quit to pursue his dream of running a motorcycle repair shop. Times have changed. My father came from the generation who graduated college, signed on with a company, and stayed for life. But today's signs indicate that your generation will have something like nine different careers—not merely jobs but careers—over the course of your life.

We are not our grandfathers, and we don't want to be. Sitting down at one desk for the rest of our lives doesn't have the appeal that it did to the generation that witnessed the Depression. But, even though I know you are right, that so many graduates never work in the fields they majored in, it feels like a contradiction to the "study what you love" concept. It feels like you are doomed to never actually do what you love.

Just the opposite. You *should* study what you love, because you'll thrive there and thus perform at your best, and because guarantees of "this-degree-equals-that-career" have a noticeably short shelf life nowadays. Which brings us to Plan B: exploration and transformation. It assumes that a far better use of college is the transformation of you as a person, a human being, who will probably have a varied career life. This approach happens to be far more true to who we are and how we are wired (which intimates it might be a far better way).

Now yes, yes, I understand that certain professions require highly specified training. Neurosurgeons need those pre-med classes and biochemical engineers need to get calculus behind them and not fritter their time away on Plato and Dickens. *However*, those doctors and engineers are still human beings, and whatever their career courses may hold for them, their first and primary task is becoming the kind of human beings that can be entrusted with power and influence. Medical schools grasped this quite awhile ago, realizing that the doctor needs not only an understanding of human anatomy but also an understanding of real human *beings*—especially suffering human beings. If they neglect their own humanity for a rigorous academic track, they don't turn out to be the kind of doctor people like to be with.

Our first and foremost task is education as human beings, not merely workers—human beings that need meaning in order to thrive.

My generation is desperate for meaning. And I mean in everything. It's hard to find a category in which some company hasn't sprung up to meet the demand for "a cause" these days. TOMS Shoes gives a pair to a child in need for every pair bought. (I've bought several from them; after about a month they get too stinky to wear in public.) Any self-respecting coffee joint—from the little guys to the corporate giants—knows that people are buying more "fair trade" (no slave labor) products, as do the chocolate makers. Clothing manufacturers have learned that by avoiding sweatshops and advertising their high moral ground, they can pull in customers; I wish more actually did what they claimed. People pay for "conflict-free diamonds"; I have a plastic-free kitchen; even bicycles can be helping those in need through World Bicycle Relief. Throw in ethical eating, which rightfully targets the destructive and inhumane system of factory farms, and I think we have covered every inch of daily life. These are my people.

A couple of years ago we were passing around books like *Three Cups of Tea, Eating Animals,* and *Not for Sale* because they all addressed what was wrong and how we could change the world. In William Strauss's book *The Fourth Turning,* he calls our generation a "Hero generation."[1] We want to change the world. The environment, helping those in need, fairness, you name it—all these things matter to us. We want a revolution to get behind. Without one, we will fill our lives with little revolutions that flare up and give us the momentary buzz of an espresso. So many of those small revolutions are held out in front of us like the answer to all our longing. Often, it's nothing more than marketing, but they are marketing to something real within us.

You have entered the Warrior Stage of a young man's life. Young men have been at the center of most of history's revolutions. Deep in your marrow lies a passion to bring down tyrants, overthrow oppression, and fight for a better world—to be part of something *big.* And why did God give you such hearts? Isn't that fascinating—why you and all your peers have a heart to change the world? Was that placed in you simply to be killed? Never! I know older folks love to look down at you over their reading glasses and say something dismissive about "the idealism of youth" and how it's high time you settle down to real life, but that is not my opinion. I don't think it's God's opinion either. That counsel comes from folks who have killed their hearts and souls in order to "get along" in the world. Christianity is all about revolution—*is* a revolution to its core—and that is why God gives young men and women passion to change the world. God gave you that heart in order that you might discover both the joy of being part of his revolution and your own unique place within it.

There is a lot of wrong to be set right in the world. Everywhere you look, the planet is bleeding, children are trafficked, slavery is on the rise, and truth itself has all but shattered. This is a time for revolution, and one of the great wonders of Christianity is the idea that you are born into your times, to set your times aright. What could be more exciting? Frederick Buechner believed that, "The place God calls you to is the place where your deep gladness and the world's deep hunger meet."[2] What could be more hopeful?

One of the happiest periods of my life was in my early twenties. Your mom and I started a theater company right out of college—not because we were hoping to be Hollywood icons driving Maseratis but because we wanted to change the world. We did street theater in Los Angeles during the 1984 Olympics—dodging security and setting up anywhere we thought we could draw a crowd in order to present short, edgy pieces about the meaning of life and Jesus Christ. We loved those years.

That's really cool; that is exactly what I'm looking for, what all my friends are looking for. You actually got to live something you were passionate about. Did you get to do that for a living?

Not exactly. Not for several years, at least. I was working as a janitor for our church, and Mom got a job as an office manager for a small high-tech company. I spent my days vacuuming, cleaning toilets, and taking out the trash; she was neck-deep in accounts receivable and employee relations. This is critical to keep in mind: your passion, your place of meaning—what the older saints referred to as your "calling"—may not be the same thing that you do to pay the bills. Jesus was a carpenter. Paul sewed tents. There may come a time when living out your passion pays the monthly rent, and you will be the richest man in the world. But getting the two confused is why so many people give up on their dreams. They do a quick assessment of their passions as "marketable skills"—or some professor stuns them with the improbabilities—and they abandon their dreams for a more "predictable" life. Which of course they end up hating, go on to develop a host of addictions, and wind up in therapy. As a counselor, I used to make a living helping them out of their despair, and the line outside my door was endless.

You are not just a "worker," an employee, or a careerist. You are a human being filled with passions and desires, and *God made you that way*. You are also a young man in the workshop of God in the training of becoming a man. Whatever else might be going on in his life, every young man is in the process of becoming a man. This is his Great Mission, the deeper stream, the far more important work than career, whether he's joined the Peace Corps or landed a marketing job in New York. You have a few lions to kill before you know you have become a man and that God can entrust you with dreams coming true. Wouldn't it make a difference if you saw these years of simple work as warrior training?

Maybe. But my generation isn't going to like hearing "you have to wait." Right now, from my phone, I can transfer money from my bank account, while reading the top news headlines, while searching for the definition of a word I don't understand and then translating it into any language (which can then be spoken aloud through the tap of a button), while texting a friend, while taking a video and uploading it to Facebook. All within a few seconds. And you want me to *wait* for something? How many years am I expected to do that?

That is the boy speaking. The boy wants it easy, and the boy wants it now. It will help you a great deal to recognize when the boy is operating—not to be unkind to him but to choose the path toward manhood. I love the phrase that is engraved in the wooden beams of Balian's blacksmith shop in the movie *Kingdom of Heaven*. It says, "What man is a man who does not make the world better?"[3] This is his bearing, his North Star as he labors in the forge of his own transformation from boy to man. The boy wants to play; he wants most of life to be recess; the man wants something higher, greater, and so he accepts the process. As Dostoevsky put it, "to sacrifice, for example, five or six years of [your] ebulliently youthful life to hard, difficult studies, to learning, in order to increase tenfold [your] strength to serve the very truth and the very deed that [you] loved and set out to accomplish."[4] That tenfold strength is worth it.

If I'm honest with myself, I'm a little embarrassed by my generation's way of approaching work—me included. If I've got my history right, in the world before the Industrial Revolution, young men felt no shame to take on an apprenticeship and work their way up until they knew their profession. But things have changed and keep changing so fast we don't commit to a particular career path because it may cease to exist when we get there. I don't know. Second-guessing every career move feels like a recipe for going nowhere. I don't want to go nowhere; I want meaning and purpose. I want to know that I am stepping into something that matters and that it is something worth doing. So did I waste college by pursuing what might not be a sustainable life path? Do I not get to step into those promises of purpose and meaning? I would happily leave my stupid job if there were something obviously purposeful, something fulfilling. So how do I find that? If the offer is only in the clouds or stuck as rhetoric, that is going to kill me.

I remember a joke my high school AP history teacher once told our class: "The science major asks, 'How does it work?' The business major asks, 'How can we sell it?' The engineering major asks, 'How can we build it?' The liberal arts major asks, 'Would you like fries with that?'" It was harsh back then; now it's haunting me.

Exploration and transformation, my son. There is a life you can love, but it takes courage, perseverance, and a little cunning to get there. It takes a warrior. You are in the thick of exploring who you are and what you are and why you are here, what the world is about and where God is moving, how and where he is moving *you*. I absolutely love what I do; my work is my passion. And I have the profound joy of knowing I'm having an impact on the world. For the most part I love my life. You can find a life you love. You can. But I didn't step into this the day after college. There was a lot that had to happen in me as a young man before God could entrust me with the life I now live.

This all sounds a bit like, "Wait. Work. Maybe life will come one day."

There is the boy again—he is filtering what I'm trying to say. I am not pushing you down with, "Just go work and maybe one day life will happen." We are reframing what this time of life is about.

There's something important you need to know about our culture—your culture. Author Robert Bly called ours a "Sibling Society," meaning a society shaped by peers rather than by elders, a society shaped by a loss of fatherhood. Adolescence is forced upon children at a younger and younger age (twelve-year-old girls now dress like coeds), while at the same time adolescence is protracted out into adulthood so that adults want to remain adolescent. Women at fifty-five show up in bars also dressed like coeds; we call them cougars, and I want to say, "You're fifty-five—act like a mature woman, for heaven's sake." A Sibling Society worships youth and rejects the rigors of adulthood; it is the world of the perpetual freshman year. Bly said the fruit is simply this: "People don't bother to grow up."[5]

Yeah, when I think about the guys I know—Michael, Skye, Julian, TJ, frankly almost all of them—I really love their hearts, but yes, it does feel like there is a lot of "boy" inside of us. The boy can be a source of wonder and creativity and spontaneous joy; but it also feels like he loses heart quickly, demands life now, and he's the one that makes us want to drink and play video games rather than doing something about our lives.

Exactly. Thus the choice before you is a bold one: to accept the wild, daring process of becoming a man.

Those hours I spent as a janitor were not wasted. I learned so much—the satisfaction of putting in a hard day's work, of pressing through tough situations to bring about a good outcome, and the rigor of perseverance—which strengthens you just as running or free weights strengthens you. I also learned how to deal with all sorts of people and their quirks. This is actually going to take an enormous amount of pressure off. The beauty of accepting the process releases you from the pressure of Be There Now.

I understand where you are headed, but this has a hint of "Enjoy the ride; the journey is the destination" stuff in there. I hope I'm wrong; that mantra is totally unhelpful, and I always imagine it spoken with glazed eyes.

I don't buy "the journey is the destination." That was made up by people who found themselves perpetually lost and needed to justify their disorientation. It is pure adolescent spin. The journey is the journey; the destination is the destination. The overnight flight to Istanbul is nothing like being in Istanbul. You've got to keep the hope of Istanbul—your dreams and desires—out there before you. Those thirteen-hour flights can be brutal if you feel like you'll never get there, trapped in an endless "journey." The heart nosedives and your biggest hope becomes the next pass of the drink cart.

Yes, of course there is a journey before you. But it has a destination: manhood—possessing a wisdom and strength that allows you to love a woman for a lifetime, be a great dad, lead a movement, rule a kingdom, and change the world. You are in the dojo of the Warrior Stage. (This is also the stage of the Lover—we'll get to that in a minute.) This season of your life began around the age of seventeen or eighteen and has now become your job in earnest. The warrior learns to master the art of holding fast to dreams while accepting the rigors of becoming the kind of man who can be entrusted with those dreams; whereas the boy's passions are undisciplined and undirected, so yes, he loses his way and loses heart easily.

One of the great enemies your generation is going to have to fight is the attitude of entitlement. Yours was the childhood where every boy got a trophy—whether they won or lost or even played in the game at all. My generation owes you all a great apology. We were so afraid of screwing it up like many of our parents did that we overindulged and weakened the race, worrying more about your self-esteem than we did your work ethic. The entitled boy feels that life ought to be easy, dreams should come true, and everybody gets a prize no matter how they perform. That boy is truly shocked when he comes to realize—often painfully—that the world doesn't owe him a thing.

This is beginning to remind me of Santiago from Paulo Coelho's *The Alchemist*. It is one of those stories that pulled me in, and I've gone back to reread it several times. Santiago is a young man who has a dream, of buried treasure to be exact, and he learns to listen to his heart and watch for signs as he follows his dream. The plot really is that simple at its essence, but I love it. Here is a story about moving in the direction of your dreams, wrestling through doubt and setback, laced with love and danger, and in the end his dream is realized.

I love the story because I want it to be true—for me. That if I move in the direction of my dreams, and follow the "omens," and fight my way through the setbacks, my life will be full of adventure and romance, and I will find my treasure. Early on Coelho gives this wonderful piece of hope in order to begin the journey—the "sage" character Melchizedek has come to the boy Santiago at the very moment he is choosing whether to follow his dream.

> "Everyone, when they are young, knows what their Personal Legend is.
>
> "At that point in their lives, everything is clear and everything is possible. They are not afraid to dream, and to yearn for everything they would like to see happen to them in their lives. But, as time passes, a mysterious force begins to convince them that it will be impossible for them to realize their Personal Legend."[6]

Earlier in their conversation Melchizedek said,

> "[They believe] the world's greatest lie."
>
> "What's the world's greatest lie?" the boy asked, completely surprised.
>
> "It's this: that at a certain point in our lives, we lose control of what's happening to us, and our lives become controlled by fate. That's the world's greatest lie."[7]

I recommend the book to folks all the time. Some of my favorite conversations I've had with friends were late in the evening, when we just started talking about dreams and how nothing could stop us from going to Africa or starting a business or opening up the first newspaper to really tell the truth. Everyone was able to let their dreams run wild those nights. Somehow, under the stars, we felt again that anything was possible. I loved those times. But, like Santiago when he gets ripped off in Tangier, we forget that feeling and doubt creeps back in when the sun rises, and I don't know many people who are moving toward the dreams they voiced those nights. I feel so bad for my friends. I want each of them to move in the direction of their dreams, before they "change" (meaning surrender) with the voice of comfort or fear. Or they run off chasing everything, anything, hoping something will come of it.

Later in the story, when Santiago is near giving up on his dream, Coelho offers another piece of wisdom: "We are afraid of losing what we have, whether it's our life or our possessions and property. But this fear evaporates when we understand that our life stories and the history of the world were written by the same hand."[8] I love that; it's so reassuring.

The reason you love *The Alchemist*—as I do—is because the story is speaking deep truth to you. It whispers a promise the heart yearns to hear: *It can be done. Life can work out. Dreams do come true.* But remember—you are watching Santiago from outside the story. What do you suppose it felt like to him within it? Probably very much like you are feeling right now—sometimes hopeful, other times confused, eventually disoriented and a little discouraged. We love Santiago because he feels like us. And notice this—when the tale begins, Santiago is an adolescent. By the story's end, he has become a young man.

These stories are like maps; the view from up high gives you the lay of the land, helps you get your bearings, but it's a very different experience looking up from the map to the world right before you—the old forest-for-the-trees thing. This is vital for us to hold on to: living *in* a great story looks and feels quite different than watching one unfold. "The way through the world / Is more difficult to find than the way beyond it," as the poet Wallace Stevens said.[9] One of the essential messages of *The Alchemist*—or *The Hobbit, The Aeneid,* any of the great stories—is this: *Do not give way to despair; do not lose heart.* This battle toward a life worth living is far more art than science. It is the art of the warrior.

I was watching a remarkable documentary on the Dorobo hunters in southern Kenya. Their bows simply aren't strong enough to bring down big game, so they steal the kill off lions. In a stunning display of courage and cunning, they walk right up to a pride devouring a wildebeest; their unwavering confidence causes the lions to run off. In the next scene the men are roasting wildebeest flank over an open fire, talking, and laughing. One of them says, "But not everybody fights lions; some people are cowards."[10] That is the campfire you want to be at—the feast of the daring.

This is going to take courage, because fear is the number one reason men give up, sell out. It will take perseverance because nothing worth having comes without some kind of fight. It will take cunning because most men-who-are-really-still-boys move into the world with a childish naïveté, ignore the lions, fail to reach their dreams, and then blame the world or God when in fact they were simply insisting that life allow them to remain freshmen forever. You have a number of lions to slay—fear is one. Despair is another. Entitlement—the entitlement of adolescence—is a third. Either you kill them or they eat you and your dreams for dinner.

Courage, perseverance, cunning—that's how you kill lions. Live that and you will have a story worth telling.

two

Bouncing Checks

I'd like to live as a poor man with lots of money.

—Pablo Picasso

The errand-runner job I took hardly seemed to be what I had been working toward in college. I took it to pay the bills—and because they were the first people to return my e-mails. Four years of higher education and I found myself returning cat food. My alma mater didn't offer a bachelor of science in that career track, but the job certainly felt like BS.

When did wanting to do something worthwhile turn into just wanting the day to be over and done with? Before graduation we used to go to the beach and talk about "swan diving" into the unknown. The ground was falling out from under us, but if we were going to be thrust into the black, we figured we might as well go down with a flourish.

It took me almost a year before I couldn't take the meaninglessness anymore. Almost a year before I stepped back out into what feels like the wild of job searching. I quit on my birthday as a nice way to celebrate, but most of my peers didn't support the choice. They looked at me like I was crazy for leaving such an easy job that paid the bills and gave me good stories to tell. For many of them, holding out for something we would have dreamed of back in college was naïve, or better still, *creating* the dream we wanted was almost fantasy. The life expectancy of dreams sure seems pretty dang short.

It all comes down to money.

I've got friends who are chasing the American Dream, friends who are opting for the new minimalist movement, and friends trying to do both at the same time. Really—I think my generation is infuriating and completely disoriented when it comes to money. On the one hand we have watched (like no generation before us) self-made millionaires spring up overnight, and I'm not talking about a million dollars. I'm talking hundreds of millions made from selling an *app*. In 2012 Rovio, the company that created Angry Birds, was worth more than $2.25 billion.[1] Some ditz can put her video on YouTube, become a one-hit-wonder, and cash in big-time by selling advertising. I know a complete knucklehead who developed an app and made $75,000 in the last month, with no end to the profit in sight.

And you know what? I can't blame my friends for trying. My job as a rabbit runner / glorified grocery shopper actually paid ridiculously well, and I was able to buy a Yamaha FZ1. Man, I loved that bike. The previous owner had turned it into a bit of a street fighter, taking off the faring and rewiring it to be the epitome of sleek, painted jet black. Flying through the canyons, I knew what

Sam Flynn felt like in *Tron: Legacy*. It sure looked to me like money buys happiness.

But then I started dating a girl who is really conscientious about money and the needs of the world. She'd rather give everything away to the homeless than buy nice things for herself. She shops at thrift stores (before Macklemore had everyone doing it) and patches up worn-out clothing long before retiring anything. This is one of those new revolutions I was talking about—the minimalist movement as a rejection of American excess, telling us to forgo all unnecessary possessions and give away all but the bare essentials. A friend was at a conference for millennials recently, and the big-name speaker said if we have two T-shirts we have one too many. This is capturing the imagination of a lot of young Christians right now.

Who's right? Is anybody right? They feel like two extremes. The first makes us believe we can be an overnight success and start toweling with hundred-dollar bills. (I just heard from my friend who developed the app; he's now up to $90,000 this month.) The second grinds out the guilt and has us dropping everything we own at the local shelter. A new American Dream or a Citizen of the World—both feel like someone ordered Rocky Mountain oysters for me. At least in the second option I can give them to my neighbor.

I hate money. But I like to eat. I want a cell phone so people can get in touch with me. I want to take Susie out on a date. I'd really prefer to sleep indoors. And to do all that I need money. My friends are selling out for money, or denying money and living like they're back in the 60s. I hate the way it messes everything up. Maybe money really is the root of all evil.

I hear you. Money is messy, and down the road when you start adding a wife and kids into the equation, money gets messy and urgent. But it's also very clarifying—I mean, nothing can sort out your priorities more quickly than money. That's what the scripture was trying to address when it said that "the *love* of money is a root of all kinds of evil" (1 Tim. 6:10, emphasis added). Money itself is not evil—greed is. Men leveled the rain forests out of greed, with no thought for the future or the ethics of what they were doing; they raped the oceans for the same reasons. Sweatshops, child labor—all those injustices that make your generation so righteously pissed—those are the result of greed. The issue is lust, gluttony, excess—that is the root of all evil. Not money. Greed.

But what about the fact that everything runs on money? I mean, it has become so natural for men and women to work soul-killing jobs until they are worn to the bone, forsaking time with family, never enjoying the world around them, in order to keep the life that everyone else has told them "matters." Walt Harrington wrote in *The Everlasting Stream*, "Years ago, I had stood in my yard at dusk, a glass of wine in my hand, and felt a rush of satisfaction for all the things I had acquired. Then I quickly worried about whether those acquisitions might someday be a trap that would force me to work at what I no longer enjoyed just to pay the tab."[2]

Money seems like a seduction that lures you into a trap, and then that trap becomes your life prison.

We don't hear about Geoffrey, the carpenter who spent his lifetime crafting chairs and tables only to scrape by; we hear about the successful, the powerful, the accomplished. One has a life that might be fulfilling but is broke and no one knows him;

the other looks glamorous and important, but I know I could never become that. You are beginning to see my frustration, I think.

That is The World you are ranting against. And rightly so. The World came up with strip malls, strip mines, and strip clubs. The World is governed by injustice and excess. But making money is not necessarily "of the world." God said, "A generous man will prosper; he who refreshes others will himself be refreshed. . . . A generous man will himself be blessed, for he shares his food with the poor" (Prov. 11:25; 22:9). One of the great joys of making money is having something to share. But you can't share what you don't have; the more you have, the more opportunity you have to do good. Some friends at church really wanted to adopt a child from overseas, but they couldn't afford it. Money can be the means to great redemption if you have it.

Let's compare The World and the kingdom of God—money is one of the dramatic places where the difference between the kingdom and The World shines brightly. The World is driven by what Aristotle called "mimetic desire." It works like this: two little boys are in a room; one picks up a ball and begins to play with it, and suddenly, the other boy wants that ball too. You see it every Christmas—there is the "one thing" everybody has to have. People get trampled on Black Friday because of mimetic desire. People "want" what other people seem to be enjoying. The entire system is built on envy and endless consumption. The World says money equals happiness, so spend your life chasing money. Jesus stepped into the madness like the one sane man in a building on fire, calmly pointing us to the exit when he said,

No one can serve two masters. Either he will hate the one and love the other, or he will be devoted to the one and despise the other. You cannot serve both God and Money.

Therefore I tell you, do not worry about your life, what you will eat or drink; or about your body, what you will wear. Is not life more important than food, and the body more important than clothes? Look at the birds of the air; they do not sow or reap or store away in barns, and yet your heavenly Father feeds them. Are you not much more valuable than they? Who of you by worrying can add a single hour to his life?

And why do you worry about clothes? See how the lilies of the field grow. They do not labor or spin. Yet I tell you that not even Solomon in all his splendor was dressed like one of these. If that is how God clothes the grass of the field, which is here today and tomorrow is thrown into the fire, will he not much more clothe you, O you of little faith? So do not worry, saying, "What shall we eat?" or "What shall we drink?" or "What shall we wear?" For the pagans run after all these things, and your heavenly Father knows that you need them. But seek first his kingdom and his righteousness, and all these things will be given to you as well. (Matt. 6:24–33)

So, then the minimalists are right—we shouldn't even be thinking about money or having "stuff."

Well, kind of. When the Scriptures tell us that if you have two coats, give one to the poor, we need to notice the math—you cannot give someone your extra coat unless you first *have* an extra coat. You can't help the poor if you yourself are poor. And wouldn't you like to do that more than once in your life? So you will need a means of procuring extra coats. If you have resources, you can do a great good. I think the minimalist movement is one of those examples of a really good desire taken out of context. As G. K. Chesterton warned,

> When a religious scheme is shattered (as Christianity was shattered at the Reformation), it is not merely the vices that are let loose. The vices are, indeed, let loose, and they wander and do damage. But the virtues are let loose also; and the virtues wander more wildly, and the virtues do more terrible damage. The modern world is full of the old Christian virtues gone mad. The virtues have gone mad because they have been isolated from each other and are wandering alone.[3]

I respect the virtue of the minimalists, but like the hippies of the 60s, this is a childish notion of how the world works. (What is it, by the way, with your generation's fascination with the 60s? It was a disaster.) Just because a movement seems humble or noble doesn't mean it represents the kingdom of God. Communism promised the working man a fair shake, but in the end it destroyed the economies of every country that tried it and the people most hurt *were* the working class. I was driving through a lovely village in Slovakia a few years ago where a friend lives. All around the town square there were empty shops. "This is where the craftsmen used to work and sell their goods," Bo explained. "Lovely goods. But communism destroyed these shops and the trades too. No one has the skills to pass on anymore. It is really very sad."

My generation thinks capitalism is bad because of all the greed. The Occupy Wall Street movement was spurred on by legitimate outrage; I didn't know anyone my age who was not excited and hopeful for the revolution. But now that legislation has passed, it is the prolonged riot that is close to illegal, not the manipulation of funds and flat-out thievery being committed by CEOs and stock managers.

No question that greed has corrupted the capitalist system. But that doesn't make the system itself corrupt. Money is like a car—it can take you good places, it can take you bad places, it can open up adventures, and it can do some serious damage. Everything depends on who's driving. People do some pretty stupid things with cars, but that doesn't make cars evil. Capitalism has proven to be the best system on earth for allowing the working class to better their lives. Look at it this way—the poor vote with their feet. Why do we have to have such strict border control with Mexico? It's not US citizens trying to go south. All over the world, the working man knows his best chance to make a better life for himself is in the United States—that is, unless we destroy our own economy.

But let's take money off the table for a minute and talk about the fruits of our labor. Money is simply the representative of our labor. We are never going to return to a system of barter and exchange—I cobble a repair on your shoes and swap it for the bread you baked this morning. Nowadays we work, in return we are paid, and we use those wages to care for our needs and hopefully for the needs of others. Money is simply the fruit of our labor, and labor is a very good thing and *very* important for men to feel like men. When God created man, it was to "be fruitful" (Gen. 1:28). The first thing Adam got was a job. There is deep satisfaction in a hard day's work. No true man wants to feel like he is a freeloader, living off someone else's labor.

One of the nastiest jobs I ever had was in the summer of my eighteenth year. I was working for the county in Oregon, blowing insulation into attics. It was 90 degrees that July and probably about 120 degrees in those attics. I sweat like a politician hooked up to a polygraph; I sweat like I had never sweat before, which caused the tiny insulation fibers to stick over every square inch of my body. Horrible stuff. But even still, when we finished the day, there was this deep sense of "Man—we did it! We pushed through something really hard. We *earned* this paycheck!"

This is essential to masculinity—putting your shoulder to the plow. Not in meaningless slavery, but as men who are here to be fruitful, who *want* to be productive. As Paul wrote,

> We were not idle when we were with you, nor did we eat anyone's food without paying for it. On the contrary, we worked night and day, laboring and toiling so that we would not be a burden to any of you. We did this, not because we do not have the right to such help, but in order to make ourselves a model for you to follow. For even when we were with you, we gave you this rule: "If a man will not work, he shall not eat." (2 Thess. 3:7–10)

I think I should probably be honest and admit that often it isn't the job that I don't like—for a long time it was work in general. I didn't get that sense of satisfaction out of work, which I chalked up to the fact that I was working small jobs. But a project last summer brought a little clarity to things. My friend Trevor and I were staining a large outdoor deck. The days were long and hot and dry, and the chemical we were using was nasty; even with face masks and eye protection we had to force ourselves to take breaks when the world started spinning and cartoon animals started dancing in circles around us. But at night, when the work was done and we sat around the poker table, we both felt that the cold drink and the camaraderie were richer because of the work we had put in to be there.

One of the best feelings I had as a young man was cutting the ties I had to you and Mom financially. I mean, I was grateful for your help in college, but I couldn't stand being dependent afterward. There is something innate in me that knows I am meant to handle things on my own. Maybe it's even a primal sense that I should be capable of putting food on the table. Whatever it is, financially standing on my own is a core need for me to feel like a man.

Right—so we have left the question of money aside and focused on labor, and we find that honest work and its fruits are very good things. This is crucial in the move from boy to man. Money forces us to grow up; it is a constant dose of reality, and reality is a gift from God. It has this marvelous way of grounding us. Dean Potter is a truly phenomenal rock climber. But now he thinks he can fly. There's the boy again. Psychologists call it "magical thinking." Philosophers have taken this so far they doubt reality even exists. Then they back their Subaru into the neighbor's tree and reality snaps them out of their magical thinking. You need to eat. You need clothes to wear. Reality shows us just what dependent creatures we are.

And that is where fear comes in. I know so many men who make choices based on fear—fear of not having money; so they take the first job they find; fear of not doing well in a field they dreamed of, so they *don't* pursue a job; fear of not finding something better or of not realizing their dreams, so they never leave a job that is killing them.

Which reminds me of a conversation I had with Blaine and Luke about fear . . . Blaine postulated that many people have a fear of swimming and as a result never go near a swimming pool. Likewise many people in the church will avoid money, pushing it off or taking a more "humble" path. He felt this wasn't so much an act of strength or godliness; rather it was an act of fear *not* to engage in the world of money. "There is only so much of the pie out there," he went on. "It is going to be spent, and I'd like to have a say where that money goes, by affirming the systems I support . . ." (I am sure it was much more eloquent than my paraphrase, but oh well).

The idea stuck, though: it takes courage to step into the world of money, and by avoiding it we lose the ability to play a larger role in saying where it should be spent.

I received a terrible phone call yesterday afternoon from the mechanic I've been working with to get my VW bug back on the road. He was delivering that old phrase I've heard too many times: "Looks like this is going to be more difficult than we thought." Immediately I thought, *How am I going to pay for this?* But he was right. It needed some serious work. And now the cushion I thought I had in savings wasn't enough to pay for it all, and whoa boy, it felt like the floor was falling out. It was a battle to stay focused on the fact that God will take care of me. I jumped to thinking of ways to take on more work and digging through old birthday cards in the hope that I missed some cash from Grandma. The overwhelming sensation was: *I'm sinking and no one is here to hold me up.*

This is what I meant when I called money a constant dose of reality. It forces us to wrestle with what we truly believe. Are you fundamentally on your own? Is it all up to you? I believe this is the heart behind the biblical idea of tithing. When you get that paycheck at the end of the month and the first thing you do is take 10 percent out to help others, you're immediately faced with, *Do I really trust God to take care of me?* That's what Jesus was getting at in the whole lilies-of-the-field thing:

> What I'm trying to do here is to get you to relax, to not be so pre-occupied with *getting*, so you can respond to God's *giving*. People who don't know God and the way he works fuss over these things, but you know both God and how he works. Steep your life in God-reality, God-initiative, God-provisions. Don't worry about missing out. You'll find all your everyday human concerns will be met. (Matt. 6:31–33 MSG)

The World says, "Chase money. Money is your security." God says, "Chase me. I am your security." When your mom and I married, we didn't have two nickels to rub together. I mean, we didn't have a *dime* in savings. All our furniture was borrowed or given to us. We ate off of a folding card table your Grandma Jane loaned us—for ten years. We shopped at thrift stores. We lived paycheck to paycheck, and those were some of the happiest years of our lives. We had a great group of friends, we loved our church, and we had a lot of fun. God took care of us. The Big Lie is that more money makes you more happy. It's just not true.

But if you don't have any money, your life can be miserable.

That is also true. Rather than "filthy lucre," Scripture looks at money mostly as a blessing from God:

> The blessing of the Lord brings wealth, and he adds no trouble to it. (Prov. 10:22)

> Humility and the fear of the Lord bring wealth and honor and life. (Prov. 22:4)

Here is the shining beauty of the kingdom. There is an "if" to that promise that all things shall be given unto you: seek ye first the kingdom of God. God will provide for you *if* you are first seeking his kingdom, living for him.

Look—either we have God or we don't. Either he is our ally, or we are on our own. What you believe about this affects everything else.

If you don't have God—and I mean as an intimate ally, right by your side—you must do your best to figure out a path for your life. This is of course how most men live. The entire world is based upon this assumption—universities, markets, career fields, economies. I have no counsel to give you here, for I have rejected that view of the world and cannot tell you much of how it works or how to outwit it. I reject the premise the whole house of cards is built on.

"There is a God; he is our Father" changes everything.

Now, let me add quickly that when I say "believing in God," I'm not referring to a casual acknowledgment of his existence. If you do have God, you must act like it. For he does not lend his help to those who take him casually—just as you don't offer the treasures of your friendship to those who take you casually. You must seek him with all your heart so that you might discover his help, align yourself with where and how he is moving, and take advantage of all he is bringing you.

God promised us, "But if from there you seek the LORD your God, you will find him if you look for him with all your heart and with all your soul" (Deut. 4:29). However, there is a condition in that promise: *if* you seek him with all your heart and soul. Most Christians forget that part, and then wonder why God doesn't seem to be more present in their lives.

Yeah, we really do. A couple of months ago I got an e-mail from a buddy of mine that said:

> I don't know how I didn't realize it before today. How could I have been so blind; so numb to my own senses? It seems so obvious to me now. How else could I explain what I have experienced here? The smell, a rancid stink that wafts in through the open doors, that they attribute to the ocean but do I detect the slightest hint of sulfur? The people, miserable souls clinging to their entitlements as if those small perks they are so used to receiving could ever save their souls. They scream and shriek, claw at the air, gnash their teeth, demand fair treatment as if they deserve it more than anyone else. It is my punishment to endure their cries and it is their sins of gluttony, greed, pride, vanity and wrath that have brought them here. All I can do is ask myself what heinous sin I have committed in my past to face a punishment this severe.
>
> I don't know how I didn't realize it before today. I work at Hell.

My reaction upon reading this? I laughed, and without hesitating a *Yep* popped up in my head. Not that his job is worse than anyone else's, but I understood that he is far from where he wants to be, where he dreams of being, but he needs to pay the bills. So what do I say to my friend? Is this just something to be endured? If we are just working to survive—or, as Calvin's father would say in *Calvin and Hobbes*, if we are "building character"—what happens to our dreams?

Obviously we've been told to chase our dreams. Over and over again every high school and college graduation speech challenged us to reach for the stars (as though they had just stumbled upon an original metaphor). But all the while we weren't given much on *becoming* the people who could handle the dream when we got there. Probably because Disney didn't think it had the right musical ring to it.

What I want to say to your friend is, "For now—just for now. You have a future; you have a Father who loves you. But yes, you are in the forge—let it strengthen you. Hang in there. God is up to something in these days—look for where he is shaping you. It will be worth it." As a warrior, you will have to fight to hang on to your dreams. As a young man, you also have to learn the discipline not to lose heart through really hard stuff. I am a successful author now, but in my early twenties I went through some pretty tough times. God is shaping us to become men who can handle life. Money actually destroys a lot of men. Money in the hands of people who are still children inside does enormous damage. So does power, fame, and influence.

Mankind has an allergy to God; we find it uncomfortable to seek him, to align our desires and our ways of doing things with his desires and his way of doing things. Agnosticism comes so naturally to us— to forget him, to accept the "evidence" that life is pretty much up to us. We are half-hearted creatures when it comes to God and his way of doing things. So he allows trial, confusion, and distress in hope that it will *compel* us to seek him. As we do, things in us are being addressed: our unbelief, our independence and self-reliance, our fear, our pride. (Better sooner than later to address these, by the way—they are the things that destroy a man's life somewhere down the road.)

The Christian is something of an amphibian. We live in two worlds—this world of men and commerce, of our times and culture. We also live in the kingdom of God. Too many Christians accept a vague notion that God is somehow at work in this world but for the most part take the world of men as the truer world and operate upon the rules and assumptions of that world.

You really must resolve this first: Do I live in a parallel universe? Is there a kingdom of God which I am a member of and can participate in? Do I have his help? If you answer yes, then you must proceed like it—seek it, learn to live within it. Otherwise you are left with, "Here is the world—it is unstable, unfair, and unpredictable. Find a way to make life work." Which proves mighty hard for most men but nearly impossible for the believer, because God is jealous over you and will not lend help to your efforts to live life at even a casual distance from him.

Notice how your heart responds to some of the basic disciplines of money: Stay out of debt. Live within your means. If you don't have enough money to buy that latte every day, don't buy it. It is the *boy* who cannot restrain himself and puts the big-screen TV on a credit card—and then pays twice its worth in interest. You don't want to become someone else's slave, and debt makes you a slave.

Yeah, it really does. I have a friend who maxes out every credit card he gets just to buy clothes and go out to fancy dinners. We call it the "rich man, poor man syndrome," like when the folks making minimum wage buy spinner tires for their minivan instead of backpacks for their kids. I don't want to be a slave. The boy in me may not like waiting for things, but the man in me knows I'd much rather live free from debt and this awful dichotomy of the rat race and the minimalists.

And the most beautiful thing of all is this: If we will reject the whole mimetic nightmare of The World, if we will align ourselves to God's way of doing things, money will not rule our lives, nor will fear. Money won't even be what we are thinking about; we'll be chasing higher things. Then our finances will become one of the main opportunities where we get to see God come through. And he loves to come through.

three

The Book of Love

*She didn't say it, I only thought she said it. So really it
was my thought, my words, and not hers. How could I
confuse "I love you" with "May I take your order?"*

—Jarod Kintz

We called it the turkey drop, and according to *Urban Dictionary*
we weren't the only ones slinging around the idiom. It is defined
as the situation of freshmen who try dating long-distance once
they enter college, who then find the appeal gone by Thanksgiving,
wherein one or the other is dumped. Thus, the turkey drop. I read
somewhere that 95 percent of long-distance couples don't make
it past the first year of college.

You know that I came to college with a girlfriend that I had
been dating for some time, close to two years, and like many
other incoming freshmen with significant attachments, my time
was torn in two. On the one hand I dove in to all the initiation

stuff—beach barbecues and section meetings. But my attention was never fully there. I was defined by a relationship that existed in the world of texting and video chat, and when other freshmen went to lunch together, I sat in my room waiting for a phone call. I didn't have much of an identity on my own; I hadn't for years. I knew that I wanted out, and shortly after my turkey drop I found myself single and happy (well, happy a month or so later).

It was only in that season after the breakup that I began to realize that I had been bouncing from girl to girl since I was twelve. As in, the most time I would spend single or not pursuing anybody was about a month. So, for the first time in six years, I decided not to pursue a girl. I wanted to know what it was like to have an identity outside a coupling. I didn't want to be "Sam and Christina" or "Sam and Liz" anymore; just Sam. But being "just Sam" took some adjustment.

I didn't realize it at first, but I had opened the door to a whole truckload of issues that were just waiting to pour out. In the year that followed, I began to realize just how much of a black sheep I had felt in our family and how much I let that define my actions. I got on medication for my mood; I drank and wandered into friends' rooms to plop down on their couches and vent all I was thinking. Meanwhile, I was head over heels for a female friend of mine—the girl no one got to date—and when I finally confessed my feelings to her, I was added to the list of rejected boys.

In reaction to being told I was not good enough—not verbatim, but by clear action and the loss of a friend—I went abroad the following semester, my junior year, and somewhere inside me decided that I wasn't going to be "not good enough" anymore. So I played with the other girls on the trip. I mean like a tool plays with girls. And quickly developed a new reputation: Sam is trouble.

I would be lying to you if I said I didn't like it.

For the first time in a long time, I was not defined by the girl I was with because I was never really with any one girl, and I was not defined as being a loser. I was trouble. "Watch out for him, 'cause he will wreck your heart."

Never being "good enough" for girl after girl is so emasculating; in the quiet inner regions of the heart, you end up believing you are just not worth it, not man enough, destined to be the "nice guy-friend" but never the boyfriend, never the lover. No wonder you decided to break out of that. No longer defined by the girl and, yet, still totally defined—simply now as the dangerous one.

To be honest, it still sounds a lot like the boy to me.

You think that does? There are a lot of boys out there, especially in the dating world. During the first week of college, our dorm's resident director pulled the guys aside and told us, "You have now entered the 'Valley of the Golden Wildflower.'" All these boys now in the meadows of college beauties started dating like fools, hopping from one shallow relationship to another. Or wishing they could.

I had a friend named Dale who avoided all women, focusing instead on his studies of ancient Greek or on his Velvet Underground vinyl collection. He wanted a relationship, even fixated on a crush all year long over this blonde in his Latin class. But he could never make a move. The whole realm of college love felt like a poorly written reality show of drama.

One of my housemates got himself in a nightmare. Everyone

around him knew it was not a good thing, even told him so, but though my friend was a good guy, he could never be the man and walk away. They would break up over and over again, but he kept going back. She had her hooks in him, and it took years before he could finally get them out. At that point it wasn't about knowing if she was healthy or not—he knew she wasn't—but he felt that he needed to be her hero and help make her healthy. He didn't have the courage to leave, but he didn't have the strength to come to terms with the fact that by staying in the relationship, no one was getting any better. Fortunately for my housemate, he was able to push through the awful experience of a breakup before things moved too deep.

I don't think it's all the boy. I think most guys down in their hearts wanted to step up and play the part of the hero, the man, but they blew it in their own way by offering too much too soon. These were the guys who knew that their girlfriends longed to be consoled, or pursued, and so—wanting to do what they knew she was hoping for—they told the girl they loved her, or made other romantic promises, and the relationship got too close. So many times it was to the wrong girl. The fortunate ones ended in tears a year later; others may end in legal documents.

Another friend really liked a girl who was a couple of years younger than him. She was playful and attractive, and she drew out his desire to "be the hero." Well, as soon as they started dating, she started acting . . . different. She went full-blown crazy after only a few days, literally stalking him and texting every hour to find out where he was, fluctuating her emotions almost as frequently in order to control him. She seemed amazing but turned out to be holding a lot of issues inside that only reared their heads when he moved toward her. He finally broke it off for good.

I feel like most guys really come down to wanting to know the answer to one question pertaining to women: What the heck is going on?

Exactly. The very question men twice your age are still asking.

The answer is simple and profound: you are a man, she is a woman, you are history. You are irresistibly and inexplicably drawn by some force field toward an alien world holding within it the ecstasies of Eden and the hopelessness of hell. This is Love 101.

I'm really not trying to be clever; I am speaking sober truth. When love is good, it is wonderful. The whole world seems to glow under the light of a golden sun. When love goes bad, the darkness covers the rest of your life; it can eclipse your heart for a long time. But of course—we are made for love. Romance matters far more than money, more than career, and even more than calling. Love is literally the heartbeat of the universe. Santiago learns, ". . . the language that everyone on earth was capable of understanding in their heart. It was love. Something older than humanity, more ancient than the desert."[1] So let's get three things straight from the start:

First, of course you want to hook up. Nothing on the planet has the power to reduce a man to a bowl of noodles like the presence of a woman he finds attractive. Femininity is powerful medicine. Try and read a book at the beach; it's mighty distracting. This isn't just testosterone and the urge to pass along your seed—that is yet another example of The World fouling something beautiful with one of its scientific "explanations." Feminine allure is soulcraft, my son. Back in the origins of our story, in the midst of a spellbound sleep, woman was drawn from our side and none of us have recovered. We've been looking for the missing goddess all our lives. You must come to terms with this: We are haunted by Eve. *By the design of God.* The guy who pretends he's not has either killed his soul or he has other things he'll want to sort out.

It isn't now nor has it ever been "good for man to be alone," meaning, without woman. A rare few may be called to celibacy, but most of us are meant to do the rest of our lives with a woman.

Second, of course it's confusing. You have more in common with an aardvark than you do with the daughters of Eve. Meeting a girl, you might just as well have been handed the code of Hammurabi to decipher. This is actually good news—you're not just an idiot, the "clueless dude." God created Eve as a mystery. How wonderful! Frustrating as the mystery can be, you don't really want to grow bored after two weeks, do you? Just when you think you have figured out women or a woman, she changes the landscape on you. Relating to a woman will forever keep us on our toes. That's a good thing, one of the reasons "make-up sex" can be wildly good. When all is predictable, men go a-wandering.

Now, by saying she is a mystery, I do *not* mean "forever beyond our understanding." Not at all. Flowers work. Love notes work. There is a *reason.* Guys will read manuals on motorcycle engines and e-trading, but never an article on femininity. Do not be like those fools. Love is going to go a *lot* better if you will learn about the feminine heart.

Lastly, you do *not* want to dink around with this. Not here, not in the arena of love. There's no casual practicing here, no driving range, no batting cages. Somebody's going to get hurt, and those hurts can be devastating. There is no such thing as recreational dating. Loving a woman is something like those guys who kayak over waterfalls—you want to get this right. When it's good with Eve, it's glorious. But there are an awful lot of divorced couples out there staggering through life like victims of a terrible accident, concussive, wondering what happened, where it all went wrong. Love matters. Human hearts matter. As we move deeper into adulthood, the stakes get higher every year.

Now that you are deep into the Warrior-*Lover* Stage, surely you have felt the growing pressure to get love right.

That pressure kicked in senior year. All the jokes about an "MRS degree" and "ring by spring or your money back" had sunk in a little more than people wanted to admit. It may sound silly, but I knew of a whole house of guys who were depressed because they were finishing up their time in college without girlfriends. Their fear probably came through the quiet assumption that finding someone, let alone the right someone, seems a lot harder to pull off in the outside world. Guys don't always want to meet girls in a bar, because it says something about the kind of girl she is, but then we aren't exactly running in circles where there are a plethora of women who seem "right" for whatever reason.

Then there is the fear of committing. One of my close friends falls into the group of millennials scarred by the divorce generation so many of my peers had for parents. Our parents—or our parents' friends, or our friends' parents—didn't fight in a jungle or take a beachhead; they fought in courtrooms. Now their children don't want to touch marriage with a ten-foot pole. Why would they? Fear drives them back from relationships, as does years of firsthand heartbreak.

And while we are talking about reasons *not* to get into relationships, does a guy need to feel established before going after the girl? Pursuing your career and gaining financial security feels like having your feet underneath you, but when does that really come? Ten years from now? Twenty? Will it ever? According to the Pew Research Center, millennials are marrying later in many cases.[2] On the other hand, it seems to me that Christian couples are marrying earlier. What are left are two different peer groups: one pushing marriage off into their thirties, the other getting married the weekend after graduation.

When is love *real* and not just infatuation? How do we move strongly toward women—and *when*?

It really feels like starting all over every time you meet someone. It's an exhausting process of finding out enough about her to see if you should date, redefining what dating even looks like, then figuring out how far to take dating before you jump ship or sail off into the sunset—which you hope is not off the edge of the world. The stakes just feel a lot higher the older you get.

I have a friend named Derek. He went to South America to teach English after he graduated from college. While he was abroad, he met a beautiful young woman from New Zealand who was also teaching. They fell fast for each other, but because she had already committed to starting a graduate program in the fall, they chose not to pursue a relationship, and when their teaching contracts ended, they went their separate ways. Well, when Derek moved home, he crashed in his brother's attic and didn't come out for a couple of months. When I talked to him the other day, he had finally moved out and started working at a farm in the middle of nowhere; he sounded just as miserable as when he stepped off the plane.

Now we are at the heart of the matter. So we have to call time-out; we have to pause the conversation because you've hit upon something critical. We are trying to answer questions about love without first settling a deeper and far more urgent matter: identity—knowing who you are, not just as a human being but *as a man*. Eve is going to test you, as you have already discovered. Until there is a settledness in you, an inner steadfastness, the storms of relationship are going to toss you around like a toy boat, maybe even sink your ship as it did your friend Derek. Let's hit the Pause button on love and romance for just a moment and push into the deeper issue of why men don't *feel* like men around women.

four

Changing the Scripts We Live By

"And what business is it of yours if I am only a girl?
You're probably only a boy: a rude, common little boy—a
slave probably, who's stolen his master's horse." . . .
"Why don't you say it at once that you think I'm
not good enough for you?" said Shasta.

—C. S. Lewis, *The Horse and His Boy*

I chose the college I attended; I recognize that I alone reap the harvest I sowed there. And it was a mixed bag. After attending a public high school, the transition into a Christian college was as much of a culture shock for me as the kids who did it the other way 'round. I knew I wanted to take a closer look at my faith, and man, the campus was gorgeous, but I had a very hard time adjusting to the culture. It felt like being dropped into Oz.

Despite signing a contract to abide by "communal standards"—

a nice euphemism for joy-crushing rules—I was busted for smoking my pipe on campus. I was caught several times sneaking into the end of mandatory chapel trying to turn in an attendance card after doing a loop through the crowd and leaving through a different door. I wrote an angry essay that was supposed to be praising "Christian Feminism" but instead focused on how forcing us to praise a viewpoint that might not be our own was . . . troublesome. (I pushed for egalitarianism or something more like that.) I got a B for straying off topic.

I danced. I drank. If the day was especially nice, I skipped class and went to the beach.

You don't need to be particularly insightful to see it coming; I ran into problems. I soon encountered the motivational "stick" this college favors: shame. Academic shame was used by professors or fellow students for poor performance—or really, anything less than "exemplary" performance. My school was a gathering place for valedictorians, it seemed. Spiritual shame was enforced by the Christian community with upturned noses or worse, the earnest approach by a spiritual leader offering "counsel": "Do you think that is the Christian thing to do, Sam? Is this what Jesus would do?" Blah!

Funny thing is, I resented them for treating me the way I taught them to see me. A phrase I heard often throughout my time at school was, "Oh Sam, you are such a lovable screwup." I was charming, so people wouldn't stay mad or disappointed with me for long, but I knew that, and I knew they thought I was as much of a joke as I felt, so I kept on behaving that way.

Whatever the form, I began to feel hedged in by shame, disappointment, and disapproval. When enough people tell you that you are a certain way, you start believing it. I did write at school, but only during my final three semesters there, and even then I wrote and coedited a page of the student newspaper that was the sarcastic, humorous, rebellious page. Now, I love being a rebel; that fighting spirit is in me for good reasons. But the rebelliousness of that page was not fueled by noble aspirations. I wrote out of the identity I had been given, and I was angry for much of it, which led to a lot of conceited and biting work that I am not completely proud of.

By the time I graduated I was pretty sure I didn't have a future in writing, despite the fact that it remained a dream to do so.

Identity is like the turning of the earth—you never really notice that it's carrying you along, but in any given moment you are actually hurling forward at 1,040 miles an hour. This is one powerful force. We cannot live beyond the way we see ourselves. When our world hands us a script, when we find ourselves repeatedly cast into a certain role, it requires almost superhuman strength to defy the gravitational pull of it. Those scripts come upon us from many circles—family, "friends," a coach, a church, our culture. I never really worried about the other stuff—what the community would have called acting out or your "rebellious phase." I knew it was your way of handling the religious suffocation, and frankly it's healthier than marching in line, letting legalism pull you under its false views of God and the Christian life. Jesus wasn't exactly a big cheering fan of the religious. But the cumulative effects of shame broke my heart because I knew that despite your strength it would wear away at you. It wears away at all of us.

The Scots pastor John Watson said, "Be kind, for every man is fighting a hard battle."[1] This was yours—the battle for your heart.

The battle to hang on to Jesus while throwing the religious out the second-story window; the battle to push through the criticism and hold true to your desires to write; the battle to cling to one of life's most important truths—that the heart is and always will be central, the powerhouse of life within us. "Above all else," the wisest man in history warned, "guard your heart, for it is the wellspring of life" (Prov. 4:23).

I imagine this is true for most universities, but this particular college really rewarded (read, *idolized*) the mind. I had many dear friends who found validation in academic performance, which then became pressure to perform again and again. It was a vortex that the best fell into and few could climb out of. No one was there to tell them their hearts mattered. No one knew to. So it should come as no surprise that in lieu of cultivating a heart that was alive and cared for, the mind reigned all-powerful, all-important, and all-consuming.

I was shocked when the powers above appointed me as an RA during my senior year. But I did have a gift with people, and I felt I could really help younger guys entering the system because of all I had experienced. I told my superiors that when it came down to my residents, their hearts mattered to me more than upholding the letter of the law. I probably didn't need to announce this, but I knew what I wanted to be about. As counterculture as it was, I believed I developed deeper relationships with my men than those RAs who couldn't see past their role as "rule enforcer." And the hearts of those young men needed some serious tending to.

One guy was so passionate—he loved the church he was in, loved the people around him, and threw himself into that world.

The sad thing is, he kept getting into tough places relationally over and over again. Somewhere inside him, there is a lot of anger and a broken tape in his head playing something like "you aren't worth much," which has played into how he relates to people and spends his time. It destroyed a lot of friendships and burned a lot of bridges, unfortunately.

Another guy was the life of the party, a ton of fun to be around and gifted with that social awareness that made every-thing he did seem cool. One time we were out for coffee, and he shared just how much pain and sadness he was living with, how his family had been torn apart by the death of his brother when he was younger, how he felt like no one knew him or cared to ask. His façade of joviality and playfulness was his mecha-nism to cope with his true belief in a horrible world filled with grief. So what if they had great GPAs? Their lives were tragic.

You simply cannot neglect the heart and get away with it. The mind is a beautiful instrument, one we certainly want to develop all our lives and not only in the college years. But God gave us the mind to protect the heart, not usurp it. As Walker Percy said, "You can get all A's and still flunk life."[2]

So let's think about identity and the heart for a moment. All men, young or old, have within them a famished craving for *validation*. It will not be denied. We will chase validation wherever we can, and we learn pretty quickly what our world rewards, what it shames, what it cares nothing about. So the athletes seek validation by being fast, strong, and winning, while the valedictorians throw themselves into papers, exams, and maintaining their GPAs. The "spiritual leader" latches on to the praise coming from their giftings, and they give their hearts and souls over to that dance, while the "cool" kids go barefoot and wear dreadlocks. We are all looking for the same thing.

When a young man doesn't know who he is and what he's made of, resisting those "scripts" that are being handed out is about the same as defying gravity. "Let's see—I gotta do my laundry, move my car, and oh yeah, I think I'll fly today."

Despite my love for the theater, I gave it up completely and entered the corporate world in my twenties, largely because I didn't think I could make it in the big leagues of professional theater. I was good, but was I good enough? I yearned for the approval of the older men in the company I was working for, and the more they rewarded my achievements, the more I gave myself over to the corporate carousel. Brooks Brothers shirts, Tumi briefcases, the whole shebang. Not that there's anything wrong with wanting a life in that world, so long as it is your calling. For me it was almost entirely based on a false self—I was simply living for what others approved of, famished for masculine validation.

But the false self—even when it is built upon some part of our genuine gifting—will never ever settle the issue inside. The horrible thing about chasing validation through money or work or women is that you can never let down; you have to keep peddling for fear of falling off.

And yet here you are—taking an enormous risk, taking up the pen again to put your writing out there for all the world to see. How do you explain that?

I feel like I'm still in the midst of it. When I first graduated, I was lost. Of course, many graduates feel lost, but I had no idea where to go next. I wasn't confident as a writer, which is what I had been driving toward those four years. So I asked a couple of guys to help me pray for guidance. Nothing was meant to be that simple, it seemed. After months of spiritual static, only two pos-sibilities were left on the table: God simply isn't going to give me "the plan" (which is where I landed) or God wants to speak to a different question. Choosing the optimistic path—that God does speak and hasn't left me out in the cold—my friends asked God what he *was* trying to speak to in my life.

This time he answered immediately: my identity.

My friends felt, and rightly so, that God was after how I saw myself. After pushing through the disappointment that God wasn't going to give me a roadmap for the next few years of my life, I asked where this was going. Their question: "Well, how do you see yourself, Sam?" *That's easy*, I thought. "I am a screwup, a black sheep, an outcast. At best I am Jack Kerouac's Dharma Bum—a wanderer who can't fit into the world, looking for answers, being reckless and misunderstood with nowhere in particular to go and nothing in particular to accomplish."

Sounds emo to me now. But I had completely bought into it, was thinking about just traveling abroad for a couple of years in an aimless adventuring way—like the Dharma Bum. Lost but looking so cool. I was living out the identity I had been handed in college.

"Okay, I see it. What now?" I asked. We prayed and asked God what he thought of me, and one of my friends got wide-eyed and started talking about *The Horse and His Boy* (by C. S. Lewis). "That was you! You are Shasta!" It took me a minute to piece together what was being implied. In that great story the protagonist is a boy named Shasta. He has run away from the cruel fisherman who raised him, and somewhere along his journey Shasta—along with the talking horse he rides—crosses paths with Aravis, a girl from a noble house. Shasta's life has been ruled by shame, so when Aravis continually refers to him as someone low, a commoner, an outcast, he has a hard time fighting it. But at the end of the book it is revealed that Shasta is the long-lost prince of a great kingdom.

Well, I hope the connection is as obvious as it was to my friend: Aravis was the voice of my peers, the voice of my college that told me over and over again that I was as low as I felt sometimes. Then we prayed and asked God to tell me who I am in his eyes. *You are my son, and a true king.* I simply sat there, not sure what to do with it all.

"Which one do you want to be true, Sam?" my other friend asked. "Do you want to be the Dharma Bum or a king?" It was obvious that I had a decision to make: accept the new identity or stay in shame. I couldn't, and wouldn't, go back to feeling like that. If the lies Shasta had been living with were the same I lived with, and once broken there was a kingdom of our own to be had, the choice was simple. We prayed. I renounced shame and the agreements I had made with "outcast and black sheep." Choosing the new identity enabled me to begin to move strongly toward a girl named Susie and toward writing. I cut drinking down to a nominal amount; instead I spent my time running, the effect of which was losing thirty pounds over the next year. I moved away from a town that, as much as a place can, had come to define me as much as the peers whom I resented.

You offered me an opportunity to write together in a project that might turn into a book, but I wasn't so sure yet. I wanted to do something on my own, but more than that I hated the kids in college who never worked for anything, the ones who joined their father's companies when they graduated without ever working for someone else. Those people sucked, in my opinion. They never struggled, so they never grew.

Six months later I was on a road trip through Malaysia when

God snuck up on me again. Out of the blue our host, David, began to ask me those "What are you going to do with your life?" questions. I talked about wanting to do something meaningful and how much I enjoyed writing. The exact same themes came up again: how living in shame doesn't do the world any good at all, how God had a nobler role for me, and if I would accept it, I could move with strength and courage into a life of purpose.

With his eyes focused on the road after having to swerve to avoid a dead monkey (yes, a freaking monkey), he said to me, "Sam, you are a king. These gifts you have were given to you to do good. How is it noble for the man in the parable who was given talents to set those aside?" I was speechless; it felt like a replay of what God had been saying to me months before. I realized that I'd been playing it safe, hanging back in the old script. It was time to accept the new one.

So here I am, and here I write.

I *love* it! This is one of those breakthrough moments every man needs—busting free of the shame and the false self, accepting a new identity (our true self), and stepping forward in courage to live from it.

I'm thinking of all those stories where the young man needs to come to terms with his true identity. In the film version of the Tolkien classic *The Return of the King*, Aragorn is a great man but he's been acting a bit like the lone wanderer, sort of a Dharma Bum. The turning point for him comes when Elrond brings him the sword of the king and declares, "Put aside the ranger; become who you were born to be!"[3] The line is repeated almost verbatim in the trailer for the Russell Crowe version of *Robin Hood*. He, too, has been living on the edges of life when he is confronted with the question, "Are you ready to be who you are?"[4]

By the way, this is the secret behind the multibillion-dollar video game industry. *Halo, Assassin's Creed, Fable*—young men get lost in those role-playing games for days because they soothe the validation ache inside. While you are in that world, you feel powerful; you *are* the hero. Your brother Luke was just playing *Reckoning*; he was a sword-wielding champion and at the moment facing two enormous ogres with war hammers. "Yikes," I said, "those guys are powerful." Luke's response as he brought them down: "But I'm powerful too."

All these stories reverberate and resound deep inside us because they are echoes of the gospel. God finds men, renames them, and calls them up into great roles. Gideon was hiding in an empty well when God addressed him as mighty warrior. Peter didn't exactly have a high view of himself, but Jesus called him a rock. Their peers thought James and John were knuckleheads; Jesus called them sons of thunder. This is the critical moment in any young man's life—we must hear who we really are, receive genuine validation, so that (like you and Shasta) we can tear up the other scripts we've been handed.

I know so many of us long for words of validation, but few ever hear them. An acquaintance of mine who lived down the street went out and bought a new (used) car one day. He spent quite a bit and took out a loan to boot. When he pulled up, he started dancing around the driveway chanting, "I own a car! Now I am a man! I own a car! Now I am a man!" I wish I were kidding. It felt pretty hollow at the time; I knew that he was getting his validation from owning things. But it's something that society had told him marks the way to adulthood.

More like killing a dandelion, isn't it? But in the absence of validation from God, we'll take whatever scraps come our way.

First we must come to terms with how we have been seeing ourselves, the role we have been playing—like "lovable screwup." This can be a painful awakening, admitting how we have been rewarded, what we have been shamed for, and how we have given ourselves over to all that. Patton was a very effective tank commander in World War II. But the accolades consumed him. As the war was drawing to a close, Eisenhower wanted to dismiss the arrogant general because of his constant outrageous comments that made the press. Patton practically groveled and begged not to be relieved of his command.[5] He couldn't let it go, couldn't separate himself from the one role where he won acclaim. Apart from "famous general" he was a hollow man.

I published *Wild at Heart* in 2001; it became a pretty big success and did a lot of good for men and women. But my subsequent books were not nearly as popular, even though I threw my heart and soul into them. It was a real test—how would I handle a disappointing reception? I had to disentangle my self-worth from what people thought of my writing. It was messy, and trust me, I had my bad days. But if my identity was built on "successful author," I think I would have simply quit, slipped off quietly, and pouted.

This can be a very revealing experience: how do we handle defeat? Because for men, it sure raises the issue of validation. If you are the compulsive student, can you take a B in a class? Athletes and competitive types—can you lose? Be ignored? Can you let go of the essential parts of your wardrobe—lose the jersey, the bro hat, the hipster look, the sports coat, the dreadlocks?

A man whose identity flows out of deep validation doesn't wilt under criticism. He enjoys applause when it comes but frankly isn't desperate for it. He can walk away from work at five o'clock; he doesn't measure his success by how much money he makes. We grow into this man, to be sure; I'm not setting a new standard of perfection. But what I am describing is not out of reach, not for any man.

We must ask God what he thinks of us. That famished craving for love and validation must be spoken to in a defining way—like he did for you. This is one of the places where Christianity really shines. God steps into the picture to help set us on a firmer foundation than the scripts we've bought into. He tells us to put off the "old man" and put on the new. He calls us his sons. He assures us we are deeply loved and chosen. Let those facts sink in to your heart, and it will set you free. Really—spend a single day holding on to, "I am a son of the living God. I am chosen. I am deeply loved." You will feel things shifting deep inside.

This sounds so simple, but it will revolutionize your life: ask God for validation *as a man*. I cannot overstate how important this is. What he brings in response will surprise and settle you. Sometimes it comes in loving words, straight from your heavenly Father. Oftentimes it comes through experiences that at first feel like hassles or fearful challenges but in fact will prove deeply validating if we accept the lions we need to face.

Earlier this spring I got a call from some neighbors who needed help trailering some horses. Now as you know, despite my childhood dreams, I am not a cowboy; I have only trailered horses a couple of times in my life. But these folks were in a tight spot and needed help, so I jumped in. Turns out they owned some very large, very anxious horses that hadn't been moved by trailer for who knows how long. It was a scary experience. I pushed through the fear, used what little skill I had—and five times that in prayer—and got those horses in my trailer and over to their new stables. A simple act, but it was for me deeply validating—I could handle it.

Do you feel that you can handle life? A woman? Your finances? Crisis when it hits? "I can handle this," is the practical daily expression of a validated man.

Bit by bit it's happening. Last summer Susie and I had the opportunity to climb Mount Whitney (tallest peak in the Lower 48) with some friends who had been planning on it for some time. We weren't sure we would be able to go since all the spots were filled, so we didn't really train for it. Then two days before the climb, the call came that two spots had opened up. I was jittery to say the least. I felt like the low man on the totem pole, the one who didn't train, who was the least athletic (or so I felt), and I dreaded the coming weekend. Shame was crouching at the door: *You're going to wimp out. You can't handle this. You won't be able to summit.*

When the climb actually came, the group decided to do the whole thing in one day; starting at base camp at 4:00 a.m. we would summit by early afternoon and be back down in time for dinner. Six hours into the climb we asked a group coming down if we were doing well, if we were even getting close. They laughed at us. We had four hours to go.

After ten grueling hours I was the first to summit. My group had been afflicted with altitude sickness, fatigue, and disorientation. By the end I was the only one who felt good enough to keep walking around on top; in fact, Susie and our friend Ryan both fell asleep immediately. At the end of the day I felt so validated, so strong. I had surprised myself and the members of our group by leading the way to the top.

Jackpot. This is why almost all initiation rituals handed down for centuries involved physical trials for young men. After finishing their training in a secret valley, the young warriors of Kauai had to swim home—miles in the open ocean. Sioux braves spent nights out on a mountain alone. For centuries the Maasai killed lions. Our elders knew that men learn by doing. It is one thing to be told you possess a genuine strength but another thing altogether to discover for yourself that you do. This is why hard work is so important for young men. If your friend could see his work in "hell" not as failure, not as a prison sentence, but as his lion to slay, he could come at it with a whole new perspective. Even if he only sticks it out another six months, he can walk away with blood on his hands and the sense of "I did that. I won. I can handle it."

Our starting place is to ask God what he thinks of us, to allow our Father to speak to us as sons. Then from there we begin to get active in the process of seeking and receiving identity and validation. God always treats a man like a man; he honors our involvement, invites our participation. Get active in the process: Where do you feel weak? Where do you need some shoring up?

"Killing lions" is all about finding validation through genuine victories fought out of our true hearts, from which we emerge with a genuine strength and sense of self. When you know you have accomplished that, it settles some important questions deep inside and allows you to move into your world with courage. The most fearsome lions will be the ones that roar with the sound of our historic shame, trying to cower us back into the false self, back to the script we were handed not by God but by The World (and ultimately by the evil one).

Climbing Whitney was a great experience in taking a risk, a risk that ended up validating me in a time when I really needed it. But it was a process to get there. I had to have the courage to step up and attempt the climb; I needed to stick with it hour after hour. Getting to the top (and back down) proved to be a series of trials instead of one simple hurdle to overcome. Maybe it's the process, the recurring demand to overcome again and again, that so many balk at. (I'm not just talking about Mount Whitney.)

Thinking back on it, I realize it has almost always been at the end of a process when I received validation. When I turned fourteen and ended my Vision Quest year by climbing the Grand Teton, you and the men of the community spoke words of affirmation over me. It meant so much to me I had to keep myself from bursting into tears. The relationships I built with my residents as an RA were a testament to the year we had spent together. When I was commended for an article I wrote for the newspaper, one that took time, and the time spent fixing a bunch of un-commendable articles I had to work through. The RA initiation backpacking trip when I led the team up a hazardous pass. The friendships forged through long nights on the beach and tears in the privacy of our rooms. The times I have felt validated seem to repeat two themes: courage and process. The strength it took to push through the fear, and the stamina to fight it through to the end—that is what made it validating.

And that is why we must reframe the decade of the twenties in a young man's life. This is the time for courage and process—the season of the Warrior, a time for accepting the journey into masculine initiation. We reframe everything by one simple choice: *I am accepting God's invitation to become a man.* From there we interpret jobs, money, relationships, flat tires, bad dates, even our play time as the context in which the boy is becoming a man. We take an active role, asking our Father to speak to us, speak to our identity, to validate us. We step into our fears and accept "hardship as discipline" (Heb. 12:7). As we do, an inner strength grows within us.

Which will change everything when it comes to pursuing a woman.

five

Back to Love, Sex, and Women

With or without you.
With or without you.
I can't live
With or without you.

—U2

You love bow hunting and fly-fishing. I love sailing. I loved it before I had ever sailed. I romanticized it to an unholy extent, imagining heading south into the warm waters of the South Pacific, with nothing but a box of cigars, a bottle of rum, and something to write my poetic gems on. The dream of watery escapism only increased with my schooling in the art of sailing. Somehow the salt in my hair and sun on my skin, the rush of fighting the waves, and harnessing the wind all combined to confirm everything I imagined sailing to be. As Steinbeck said in *The Log from the Sea of Cortez*, "This is not mysticism, but identification; man, building this greatest and most personal of all tools, has in turn received a boat-shaped mind, and the boat, a man-shaped soul."[1]

As graduation approached, I hatched a plan with Chris, a fellow English major and friend, to take his family's sailboat in Washington and sail south like Steinbeck. They had a 26'-er, and we flaunted our dream to everyone who asked what we were going to do after graduation. Thinking back on it, we had multiple occasions of unsolicited advice wherein people told us to bring a weapon to fend off pirates and the homeless of the sea; add to this the fact that neither Chris nor I had any idea how to sail, and there was a distinct possibility we would need to be rescued by SEAL Team 6. Put together we couldn't have told you the difference between a jib and a boom, let alone put out to sea.

I learned to sail because of Susie. I never would have learned if Susie had not called the sailing company and forced me to sign up. She has that characteristic *push* that I have come to deeply appreciate.

We started dating two months before I graduated, and I'd like to point out that no, I was not freaking out about graduating without finding my wife. Those early months were a whirlwind of excitement and joy and, to stick with the sailing theme, some seriously rough water. Frankly, it was nothing short of a storm. This was largely because I was sorting out who I was and where I wanted to be headed with my life, which a lot of our relationship hinged on. Susie wanted to know who I was going to be about as much as I wanted to know it, and unfortunately, it took her dumping my sorry . . . "behind" before I began to step up and play the man.

We had been dating for several months, and frankly it wasn't a pretty sight when she read me the letter. Yep, an actual letter. It was brutally honest and named my aimlessness, my lack of initiation, how I had hurt her, and how she deserved better. She was right, of course, and I love the effect she has had on me since. In addition to sailing we have been running together, adventuring, climbing mountains, reading books, and learning to love each other well. I know I've also had a dramatic effect on her, in her pursuit of knowing and caring for her own heart, which was a new category. I'd like to think I've helped her to slow down on occasion and embrace rest and affection in ways other than accomplishment.

I wasn't so sure about Susie when you first met; Mom and I only experienced her in person on two separate occasions. Plus, you kept vacillating about the relationship so we didn't know what to think, really. But when she broke up with you, for the reasons she did, Susie won my everlasting respect. Not that I wanted the pain it brought you, but I loved her courage and how she called you out. I loved the effect it had on you. Most young women just won't risk that with the man they are dating, for fear they'll lose the relationship. Like a girl who pretends she doesn't hear bad noises coming from under the hood of her car, they push their valid concerns aside, quieting their consciences with thoughts like, *He'll change once we get engaged or when we get married.* That rarely comes true; about as often as your car magically fixes itself.

So a quick word of advice: marry the man or woman *for who they are now*, not who you hope they will become.

Are you better because you are together, or are you both stuck in the stagnant water of complacency? That is the first good test for every relationship—especially dating relationships. Is your effect on each other life and a growing maturity and wholeness? Does she move you toward the man you want to be, and is your effect to bring out her best and brightest self? I love the line toward the end of the movie *As Good as It Gets*, where Jack Nicholson confesses to Helen Hunt, "You make me want to be a better man."[2]

I can't say Stasi and I were good for each other when we first met; we ran with a rowdy crowd in high school and when we went our separate ways in college, I think it was for the best. Certainly it was for her; I had a lot of growing up to do. But around the age of twenty we came back together over our newly discovered faith in Jesus. Now, what typically happens is that one partner in a dating relationship has the more serious faith, and the skeptic eventually pulls the believer down. (Thus the failure of "missionary dating." It just doesn't work.) But Stasi and I propelled each other forward in our faith, our dreams, and that was the foundation for the beautiful romance that ensued.

You and Susie have discovered that you really are better together than you are apart; that is, your effect on each other is growth and goodness and becoming your better selves. Dating is for the purpose of getting to know the person well enough to know who they truly are and to see what your effect is upon each other. We all put our best foot forward when we meet a potential guy or girl. You don't know if they're crazy or booby trapped until you get to see behind the scenes. You want to see them in social settings, with their friends (do they have friends?), with their families. It's probably even more important that your friends get to see her for who she is and how you are together. Love isn't simply blind; love is delusional. We lose half our brains, go comatose toward glaring issues, and that's where our friends can step in. I've known too many folks who make excuses for their partners and then regret it five years into the marriage.

I have wondered if "courtship" is a relic of the past, and if it is helpful to date casually in order to meet people and develop relational skills, or should we follow the trend of forgoing dating altogether? There seems to be no limit to the screwed-up ways people date. Many of my friends, me included, were at one point or another chasing girl after girl only to move on, sometimes hours after catching their crush of the week. In high school I dated a girl because it would improve my social standing. I knew a guy in college who proposed to a young woman because it made sense "financially." Real romantic. What about the couple that spends all their time on the couch in his room and only leave because they don't have a nasal feeding tube?

Our generation has grown up with leaps in technology, and as such, texting and online communication are critical pieces of many relationships. I love being able to communicate with Susie throughout the day, but the negative side would be when the couple realizes they don't engage in the real world anymore. A friend of mine experienced this in a long-distance relation-ship. They would talk online or on the phone regularly, until it hit him that they weren't *actually* living life together—none of his friends knew her, and it wasn't long before it fell apart. Tied in closely with the false transparency technology brings has been a hyperawareness of our status in relation to friends and even society. (Facebook "status updates" are most often about relationships.)

So, now that I am in this relationship myself, I can't help but think, *Whoa.* Let me clarify a little—there is the "whoa" of being tied to someone else, then there is the "whoa" of her beauty, but right now I am talking about the "whoa" of, *what on earth is going on?* I have in my phone a message I saved when Susie and I were dating, though it could have happened at any point in time. The conversation is all Susie and goes like this: "Honey, I'm not a feeler. I mean I am a feeler, but my emotional response is a little weird because with all these emotions swirling around it gets so confusing so then I just cry, and it's only later that I realize 'oh, that was joy' or 'oh, I was mad.' This is just something you need to know about me."

Oh good, I thought to myself. You can imagine how humorous I found this message and also how little light it actually shed on what is happening in the internal world of women. Even *she* doesn't know sometimes!

Truly, how different she feels from me. I can be a very social person, but at my core I draw my energy from being alone, which I suppose makes me an introvert. Anytime we would go downtown or head over to a friend's place, my internal clock would start counting down the minute I walked in the door. Susie, however, would make a new best friend every time and want to stay until Christ came back. She isn't just different from me; she is quite probably my opposite. In some ways it feels like the more I give, the more she needs. I am completely convinced at this point that we use a different set of connotations for the language we speak. It's amazing how much we can misunderstand each other.

Really, I think we all want to know what love looks like going forward. Even when I am feeling strong, living out of a good place, this thing has its good days and its bad, and they all feel completely arbitrary. I love what I've gotten myself into, but I could use some help over here understanding the heart of a woman.

I'd love to share what thirty years of marriage (and twenty counseling young people) has taught me. But let me begin with a question: What is your greatest fear, as a man?

That's easy; I fear feeling like a fool. I fear and hate it above everything else. *Hate* might not even be a strong enough word; *loathe* may be better. I hate walking into the bank and having the teller raise an eyebrow in pity when he asks my monthly income. I hate going in to buy a suit and being chided and coddled by the staff who assume I know nothing. So what if I don't know my measurements? I have cringed days after being caught in a bluff by someone who knows what they are talking about, and then calling me out in front of everyone. There are times when I feel Dean Koontz hit it on the head: "Humanity is a parade of fools, and I am at the front of it, twirling a baton."[3]

There is something about heights that makes my stomach drop, something about walking face-first into a spider web that gives me a crawling sensation all over, something about narrowly missing a collision on my bike that sends ice up my spine. But more than anything else, I hate feeling like a fool around a woman. I think most guys do. The sensation afterward is something akin to a personal black hole opening up inside my chest, and I wish it would hurry up and swallow me whole.

There was the time I took a girl to the movies, and when I asked for two tickets, the agent informed me that it wasn't even showing that day. I didn't know what to do and just stood there, frozen. Or when I took flowers to a girl at school and kept them in my backpack, and when I pulled them out, they had completely wilted. There is nothing worse than bumbling my way through a conversation where I am anything but suave. I once tried showing off on a diving board by doing a double front-flip but ended up hitting the water face-first and giving myself a bloody nose. Almost every guy I know tells stories of spectacular failed attempts at a date or an introduction or a kiss, and while the stories are told in a circle of laughter, every man's eyes go a little dim as he relives the memory.

Yep. Every guy reading this just said, "Yep." But the women didn't, at least not in the same way. Women don't shudder at stopping to ask directions, don't feel like a complete idiot when they can't get their cars started, don't feel like a total failure as a human being simply because they need someone to come alongside and lend a hand. Guys *hate* being in that position, because it screams, "I need you to bail me out *because I can't handle my life.*" Women understand we are here to help one another; they have a far more relationally connected way of approaching the world.

Men don't play with each other's hair. We don't call one another in order to talk through the details of another guy's new relationship and how their date went last night. Men aren't buying *People* magazine. When men text each other, one short message followed by an equally brief reply is enough (no emoticons, exclamation points, or "I love you!"). Our first question when meeting another guy is typically not, "How *are* you?!" but "Hey—how's it goin'?" or "What's goin' on?"—questions focused on *activity* rather than relational interdependence. Men come at the world from a conquest standpoint, but women approach life from a relational viewpoint. That's why they don't feel diminished by needing someone to lend a hand; they have a far more communal way of living.

Now, if the secret fear of men is failure, the secret fear of women is abandonment. This is *so* important to know about a woman's heart. In the core of her being is this voice that whispers to her, *I am not enough. I am too much. If he really knew me, he wouldn't stick around.* Though we all put our best foot forward in dating, we are wearing different shoes, so to speak. Guys do it so they don't look like a fool, and women do it so they won't be rejected. Start with our core fears, and you can learn a lot about the internal world of men and women.

Some people fear that admitting the deep and remarkable differences between men and women will hurl us back into the 1950s, fling doors open to discrimination, take away the vote. I believe it opens the door for us to better love one another. The same folks who cringe at the mention of gender distinctions will tell you the next moment how arrogant it is for you to assume that your friend from Palestine looks at the world the way you do, that the rest of the world speaks English as their first language, or that when they do use English, they understand the words to mean precisely what you mean them to be. Poetry translated from one language to another always loses something essential; if you want to experience what the poet meant, learn the language he or she was writing in. This is humility, not discrimination.

If we approach this from the viewpoint of wanting to understand one another, and therefore better love one another, I think we can avoid stepping on landmines. Paul prayed that our love would "abound more and more in knowledge and depth of insight" (Phil. 1:9). Stasi is not a man; I cannot relate to her as a man. We don't look at money, or family visits, or sex anywhere near the same way. When

I say, "Can you wear a different dress?" I need to remember she probably hears, *He thinks I'm ugly*, when all I was saying is that I like the blue one better.

We learn about our differences in order to be better lovers.

A woman wants to be chosen; she wants to be wanted, she fears rejection, and above all she fears abandonment. When I make plans without consulting Stasi, it sends a message that goes something like, *He is completely happy living separate lives; it doesn't really matter if I am a part of this or not.* I may have been simply trying to slay a lion, but she feels it as separation, as a form of rejection. Conquest versus connection. Surely you have begun to experience this.

I feel like I blunder into success as much as I blunder into downfalls. That Susie really values connection. That I think the world of her, and she receives love in a completely different way than me, through words both written and spoken. And that she has a really hard time believing what I think of her.

Exactly. As you get to know a woman, you want to know her story, the things that have shaped her, because you want to know who she really is. Where did she experience shame, and for what? Where did she experience being prized—and for what? Because everything you say and do is being filtered through her way of seeing the world.

You can bet that girl who was passed around sexually by multiple boys growing up doesn't really like sex, because it got intertwined with the message of, *No one really cares for you as a woman, as a human being; they just want to use you. All you are good for is being used.* Then, later in marriage her husband wonders why she doesn't desire sex the way he does. Whereas the competent, independent achiever might in fact simply be fortressing herself against rejection by hating anything in herself that feels vulnerable or feminine. What looks like strength might simply be a moat and drawbridge.

Remember—whoever she is, she has a false self too, constructed to avoid rejection and win approval. The girl you described as going "full-blown crazy" on your friend—she was flipping from one personality to another based on the cry, *Just tell me who you want me to be, and I'll be it.* The purpose of dating is to learn which is the false self and which is the true self so that you know if you really are better together. As you move into a committed relationship and on into marriage, you want to fight for her true self to come alive while being careful not to step into the booby traps of the false self. So you must know the things that have shaped her—what was she rewarded for, if anything? Where did she experience fear, or wounding, or full-blown assault?

And may I say that as you get to know her story, you want to pay *very* close attention to her relationship with her father and how he handled her heart. Their relationship will prove to be something of a Rosetta Stone for just about everything else—her personality, her fears, whether or not she believes you when you pay her a compliment, and what trips her into rage or silence. Does she have dreams for her life, separate from a need to perform? Does she take care of herself? Does she even like herself *as a woman*? What is her capacity to receive love and rest in the security of the relationship?

Back in your freshman year, when you decided to form an identity apart from a girl, I remember you admitting you were historically attracted to girls who were frankly a little crazy. Three years later you found Susie; how did you know she was different, a really healthy young woman?

I knew Susie was a whirlwind when I met her. She was fast paced and driven and spontaneous. But I knew that she wasn't just another dramatic girl because of several reasons, beginning with her self-awareness. She knew where she wanted to be going, what she wanted out of a relationship, and when she dropped all of her expectations on me after one day of dating, it knocked me off my saddle, for lack of a better expression.

But that was just it. Susie wanted good things; she wanted a healthy relationship, a Christ-centered relationship. And I could tell it wasn't an act because of the world she had created for herself. All you need to do is look at her friends, the people she surrounds herself with, how she interacts with strangers, where she is comfortable and where she isn't. It is the true litmus test to see if she is healthy. We all create worlds for ourselves that show who we are at a deeper level, much more than our "personalities." Even after one date I could tell that she was different, that she was solid.

Now, there were other girls who seemed a little like Susie from first glance; they were dynamic and exciting and beautiful. But their self-created world, their friends and their effect on others, was more like a whirlpool. They would pull people in and control them through their actions, making everything revolve around them, and when you got to the center it was suffocating. Those girls are more like drowning women than anything resembling a healthy, independent woman.

And I think it's those "healthy" indicators that help a young man know when and when *not* to come through. If a girl is basically secure inside, if her fundamental reality is, *I am loved, I am okay*, then you are free to move toward her when she needs rescue. But if she is not healthy—if she is looking to you to make her feel loved and okay as a human being—then you dare not play God for her. Though her present crisis might shout, *Come through for me*, she needs God, not you. This will really help guys with the wanting-to-be-the-hero thing, because that is a great part of us; but when do we let it move us and when do we hold back? Does she have a healthy world? Friendships? A life in God? Your friend who broke up with the girl who was always creating crises did the loving thing, because what she needed was not a man but a sure foundation in God.

All this gets really messy when things get physical. I know, this topic has seen too much attention from the pulpit these days, but seriously—there is a false intimacy in over-sexualized couples. For all of the complicated reasons that people choose to step into these waters (often some combination of affection, security, and thrill), when couples get too physical, they really do lose something. I've seen some use it as a stopgap for relational issues that never get solved; in other cases it has eaten away at the trust in the relationship. The question may or may not get asked but it goes something like, "Is this really as intimate as we've been led to believe?"

I remember a metaphor you told me once: that being intimate with someone is like gluing two pieces of paper together . . . when you pull them apart you get little tears and holes that rip and stick to the other. They are never the same and carry a little of the other with them.

And I'm not just talking intercourse; I know too many guys who operate by the letter of the law and do everything up to "having sex," but in reality that has a serious effect too. It's nothing but cheap semantics. Couples that do this often don't grow like they should, they cut out other people from their lives and subsequently their world becomes smaller and smaller, and they don't address issues in their own relationship and become hollow as a result.

This applies to couples that just make out, too, though how they stay there is beyond me. Sexuality has become such a game of walking the razor's edge between being "PC" and holding on to values that feel as arbitrary as our grandparents' curfew. I want to say that sexual intimacy *matters*. I've seen it destroy relationships all the time. But I also want to say that it doesn't just matter because someone said so, even if that someone was your parents' pastor. It matters because of the heart.

Frankly, if all you do is sit on the couch, that should probably come to an end as well. Exploring life together is everything. One of Susie's favorite lines of poetry is from Mary Oliver's "The Summer Day": "Tell me, what is it you plan to do / with your one wild and precious life?"[4] A relationship should be both wild and precious. Seek adventure. Explore. Rest in beauty. Not doing so is ignoring that which makes you both come alive.

That's a beautiful way of putting it.

A good man wants to take care of the heart of his woman. This is why it is so important for young men to understand what they are communicating when they kiss a girl, how it is affecting her *heart*. My goodness—holding hands is an enormously romantic experience for a woman. A guy might just think it's nice; a girl may well be swept into a scene from a movie. If you don't want to mess with her heart, you'll be careful what you are communicating through physical connection. In the movie *Jerry Maguire*, Tom Cruise's character has a beautiful young woman as his professional assistant who secretly adores him. After their first date, they climb between the sheets together, and he says, "This is going to change everything." She replies, "*Promise?*"[5]

Taking care of her heart and taking care of yours will also give guys a whole new framework for thinking about masturbation and porn. It's not just, "Hey—stop it." They are issues of the *heart*. I don't want to give my heart there because I want my heart free and whole, and because I want to be totally present as a friend and a lover. When I turn to masturbation, I'm turning away from relationship. When I lust over a woman's body, I am in that moment turning away from *my* woman. I want the real deal—the wild and precious gift of being in love and offering a strong love, a man's love to a woman.

That really shows the difference between love and infatuation: when you are thinking more for her benefit and loving out of a desire to see her thrive . . . when it is selfless *and* the relationship can stand without the physical, then I think you are on to something more.

All this feels really huge, but then I have to ask: Should you have killed a lion before you commit? Many traditional cultures like the Maasai require a young man to prove himself before he can marry or own land. He needs to kill a lion, so to speak. It seems wise. What do you think?

I am a big believer in having a vision for where your life is headed before you get engaged. You don't have to land the Big Job or own a house first, but when you ask a girl to marry you, what are you inviting her into? A proposal is not just, "Hey—we like hanging out together. Let's do it 24-7!" (Or more often than not, for committed Christians, "We want to have sex—let's get married!") A proposal is an invitation into a shared life—so fellas, what exactly is that life going to be about? That girl has a right to know where you are headed, cowboy, before she just up and rides off with you. Mom and I shared in the adventure of the theater company we were starting; we knew this was the city we wanted to be living in; we loved the church we were committed to; and we had a healthy community around us. I don't think a young man should marry hoping that once he does, everything else will just sort of fall into place. When she broke up with you, Susie insisted that you address your aimlessness.

Back to what we were saying earlier—one firm foundation you *do* want to have going into a committed relationship is a good sense of your identity. Your fiancée or wife cannot resolve that for you—nor can you for her. This is something you want for both of you—you want your fiancée to have the opportunity to settle some of the deeper issues of her heart and her identity before you marry, and you want some sense of who you are as a man. Now there is grace here; you don't have to have everything figured out. God loves beginnings. Adam and Eve needed each other to live the life he had for them; so much of the joy of young lovers is discovering together all that God has for you. Don't picture yourselves as architects coming in with a complete blueprint, but rather as adventurers, trying to decipher a treasure map together.

six

Decisions, Decisions

Do not fly so high with your decisions that you
forget that a decision is but a beginning.

—Søren Kierkegaard

When I was a boy, I loved the Choose Your Own Adventure books. At the end of the page you had a choice to make, usually something simple like "Do you climb the mountain even though it looks stormy, or do you head back to the cabin?" and depending on your choice you turned to a new page. I think the appeal for me was having immediate results for my choices. That and being able to peek at what would have happened if I went the other way. I died a lot in those books, come to think of it, and I can't always say it was because I was living on the edge with my choices—sometimes I just wanted to see what would happen if I chose *not* to put on the parachute. They weren't always the most creative with their endings. Pretty morbid reading for youth fiction, but hey, some crazy stuff gets printed nowadays. Later I shifted to those "role-playing video games" we have mentioned, which gave a heightened range of believability.

But life isn't as obvious as those books, with the ability to turn back a few pages. It's not as simple or always as exciting as a video game with so many reset buttons. In the past six months I have been faced with the following decisions: Should I move down to a friend's place in San Clemente to save money and get out of town? Do I need to sell my car and buy a better one, and if so which one? Do I need to get a credit card? I don't have one yet, and several people have told me I need one to start building credit (whatever that is). What kind of work should I be looking for now that I quit my last job? The biggest, most daunting decision facing me was this: Do I ask Susie to marry me? Is now the right time? And, what does that mean for our future if I do?

Sometimes I wish I had what Melchizedek gave Santiago in *The Alchemist*, just before he set out on his journey.

> "Take these," said the old man, holding out a white stone and a black stone that had been embedded at the center of the breastplate. "They are called Urim and Thummim. The black signifies 'yes,' and the white 'no.' When you are unable to read the omens, they will help you to do so."[1]

I think they would get ground to dust pretty quickly if we had them. But we don't, and making a decision can feel like a shot in the dark. Instead, I have . . . a computer: my personal looking glass into the circus of information and possibilities.

I've spent a lot of time in front of a computer screen looking for jobs and grad schools. Most everyone since the turn of the century has devoted time to the glowing god. But I have spent *hours upon hours* digging through the torrent of information trying to find answers. I am not sure how my grandfathers found employment. Probably by just walking in the door somewhere or through a mutual friend. These days I wade through online web postings and alumni connections. I have poured over listings and online reviews and search engines for graduate programs. The only real difference I noticed between the online search and the massive convention I attended in Chicago was the noise level. "We live in the age of information," says the old recording of an announcer in my head; so why does finding direction feel like a parade of hopeless metaphors? I'm drinking from a fire hose and snorkeling through mud. I've been handed a spyglass and told it holds the key, only to gaze through and find the chaos of a kaleidoscope.

More information doesn't seem to help. I feel like I'm drowning in it. I just learned how to tie a shemagh, found the best noodle bar in the Minneapolis–Saint Paul airport (Shoyu), and discovered twelve tips to the ultimate workout (it always involves buying something, which is weird). When I look for a job or try to map out my dreams, or some other future-oriented activity, somehow it almost always feels futile eventually.

I've tried making pro-and-con lists, but they have taken me nowhere. Realistically, I was only guessing as to the obvious benefits and consequences, but I doubt I had any real idea what I was actually weighing. Once I made a timeline of several possible future paths, like I was trying to peek at my own Choose Your Own Adventure. It was much less exciting, and when I dug it back up the other day, almost nothing had panned out like I thought it would.

Every so often, as the threat of becoming stagnant creeps in, I'll ask myself, "What are my dreams? Where do I want to be in five years?" as though it will give me a clear picture of where I want to be moving. It always fails for one reason or another. The answers that spring up feel too vast or too vague; how does "change the world" or "live an important life" or "write" or "do something innovative and exciting" map out what to do this afternoon or tomorrow or the day after? I get stuck in the broad, the vast. I feel like I am in the middle of a desert with no discernible features in any direction and no clue which way to start walking.

Up to the point of college, the biggest decisions we were forced to make were between home economics and outdoor sports as an elective, or white and brown rice at Chipotle. Now every choice affects our careers, our relationships, where we live, how we will survive—and each one feels more weighty than all those before it.

Yes, it feels that way. The twenties sure feel like the decade of decision making, don't they? Money, jobs, women, love, revolutions, dreams—everything we have been talking through is going to require some serious and sometimes constant decision making on your part. And though I feel our decisions are weighty, they aren't nearly as overwhelming as they feel when we are faced with them. I have never found pressure a good motivator for making decisions, nor found decisions made under pressure to be particularly good ones. So let me first try and lift some of the pressure off the decision-making process.

Your generation has been inundated with the promise that, "You can do anything." The cliché is a staple of every graduation speech, as you said, but it began far back in elementary school with good old Dr. Seuss:

You have brains in your head.
You have feet in your shoes.
You can steer yourself
any direction you choose.
You're on your own. And you know what you know.
And YOU are the guy who'll decide where to go.[2]

Heady and exhilarating stuff for a first grader. The college graduate begins to lose the jaunty promise and feel the weight of decision making descend. A limitless universe of options is not a gift, not even an opportunity to dream; it is overwhelming. Paralyzing. And untrue. You can't do everything. The future is not an endless horizon before you; you cannot simply head off in any direction. Given who you are and how you're wired, Sam, you will never, ever be a professional baseball player, concert cellist, orthopedic surgeon, mathematician, or member of parliament. You get my point. The list is actually quite long. When you consider your age, your situation, your gifting and training, the country in which you live, the economic forecast, I think you'll find that the horizon is not nearly as vast as you have been told—or as the Internet makes it seem.

The truth is, the options before you are limited *and that is a great relief.* The open ocean is beautiful to look at, but terrifying if you have to navigate it in a small boat. But you are not facing the open ocean. God puts us within a context, with a limited gifting and limited resources, and that is immensely kind.

You know, this actually sounds discouraging, like you are taking away from the bright future of possibilities. You sound like a naysayer.

Not at all. When Jesus said, "Broad is the way to destruction . . . narrow is the path to life," we don't recognize it for the relief it is (Matt. 7:13). A road as vast as the horizon is no road at all. If you were driving from New York to Los Angeles and the road before you was twenty miles wide, you would wander back and forth for weeks, turning in wrong directions constantly trying to find your way. Now add the chaos of hundreds of thousands of other motorists trying to do the same. Of course the broad way leads to destruction.

Columbia business professor Sheena Iyengar conducted some well-known research on consumer choices—how folks respond to the myriad of jams and jellies on a store shelf. Given five to choose from, people make a choice, but given twenty-five to choose from, they simply walk away in indecision, with no jam at all. She said that "in reality" people find "more and more choice to actually be debilitating."[3]

Do you recall our trip to Buenos Aires? The main road through downtown was called Avenida 9 de Julio; it is the widest avenue in the world—up to seven lanes running in both directions. Picture yourself as an ant trying to find his way home using so broad a path. This is the psychological effect of telling the Internet generation, "You can do anything!" It simply isn't true. When you begin to factor in decisions based on reality, opportunity, finances, and the constraints of love, I think you will find the road to life refreshingly narrow—that is, a path you can actually follow.

A friend of mine gave me the book *Man's Search for Meaning* by Viktor E. Frankl. In it Frankl recalls his firsthand experience of the Holocaust, and one of the things he comes to believe is this: "Everything can be taken from a man but one thing: the last of the human freedoms—to choose one's attitude in any given set of circumstances, to choose one's own way."⁴ Personally, I agree with the sentiment. I wouldn't want to believe that everything was predetermined. Because at the end of the day I am a pragmatic, and I need to function like I *have a choice*, no matter how difficult it is to make.

Me too. Pascal called it the "dignity of causation." Our choices do matter. The truth is, as helpful as Urim and Thummim might be, they are a degrading Vegas-style approach to decision making. A man wants to feel like his choices matter. By saying I do not believe your choices really are limitless, or even vast, I do not mean to say they are not weighty. Our choices are weighty. While traveling through Eastern Europe a few years ago, I was approached by a priest earnest to know more about learning to hear the voice of God (I had lectured on the topic the previous evening). He pulled me aside and through an interpreter confessed that his means of decision making was a dice (or die, for singular), which he painted red and green on varying sides. He would ask God a question, then roll the die for the answer. Sort of a homemade Urim and Thummim, I suppose. But to be honest, it felt desperate and frighteningly unreliable.

You do not want to gamble with your major life decisions. You do not have to. I think the yearning for stones to throw comes out of that place in us that feels overwhelmed. We feel once again that life is up to us; we forget we are sons and feel in the moment like orphans. "You are on your own," as Dr. Seuss said. But just like finances or women, the decision-making process has a reality to it, and "rules" to follow, which if we will accept can turn the whole thing back into an adventure with God—not a kaleidoscope of confusing images.

Our adolescent culture really does play into our confusion; with so many answers supposedly on the other side of our keyboards, we often won't ask for counsel, and even more often don't want to ask anyway. I have found myself swinging between being impulsive and being immobilized, and from what I've seen I'm not alone. If the choice is up to us and no other guidance is forthcoming, the only natural response in a culture of "instant gratification" (read, *impatience*) is either to jump at something, anything, or to never jump at all.

Those that don't jump usually have found some kind of escapism by creating a small world that they feel safe in or by sinking into the imaginary worlds of TV shows and video games. Avoiding that, we might hitch our wagons to the latest revolution, simply wanting to catch some of the momentum and meaning it seems to offer. If all we are doing is spending time and energy on a product, not stepping into something we believe is right for us, it is only a matter of time before all that is left is buyer's remorse.

Remember, we are reframing a decade. Exploration and transformation. As Kierkegaard said with such kindness, "Do not fly so high with your decisions that you forget that a decision is but a beginning."[5] Your decisions are meaningful, but not irrevocable, especially in your twenties. Tattoos at this point are probably the only irreversible decisions. The wonderful thing about the twenties (and thirties too) is that if you don't like the path you've chosen, you can change it. I chose a direction toward Washington DC at twenty-eight; I left it by thirty-one, went back to grad school (nights and weekends), and made a total course correction by thirty-five.

Take a deep breath. Let's talk about the *process* of decision making.

You are choosing the road less traveled by choosing to leave adolescence behind. You are countercultural already! Maturity grows as we accept the constraints that are before us—the boy will never be an astronaut. You will never work in medicine. Even more importantly, let us remember we are sons. God really does have a path for us if we will seek it with all our hearts. So let me offer a few questions/categories I have found immensely helpful when I'm trying to get clarity:

Am I doing something impulsive?

The boy never wants to wait, and he can get us into some real trouble. Impulsiveness can be fun, but impulsive decisions are about as reliable as a weekend in Vegas. It takes courage to wait for clarity, especially when everyone around you is rushing off to join the Peace Corps, fight trafficking, take an internship in DC, or record their first album. Sex and tattoos are notoriously impulsive. But so is choosing a major, quitting a job, or joining the armed forces. As C. S. Lewis said, "Perfect love, we know, casteth out fear. But so do several other things—ignorance, alcohol, passion, presumption and stupidity."[6]

Save your impulsive decisions for shoes, restaurants, and cannonballing into waters of unknown temperature.

Is this wise?

A difficult thing to know at your age. Wisdom is gained almost exclusively by living many years. But you can *borrow* the wisdom gained by those who are older than you. How many people have you asked for counsel? It takes humility to ask advice. Young men are renowned for wanting to make decisions on their own, but that is the first sign of a lack of wisdom. Which brings me to . . .

What do my friends, family, mentors think?

Guys come under a lot of false pressure trying to figure life out on our own. This is where femininity sails past us—women are far more likely to ask for advice. Breathe the fresh air of knowing you never were meant to make weighty decisions on your own. I find it fascinating that Jesus spent an entire night in prayer, alone on the mountain, before he chose the men who would be his twelve closest apprentices. That's really freeing—not even the Son of God tried to figure life out on his own.

Despite a fairly decent GPA, I got kicked out of high school because I continually skipped class. Once free, I never intended to darken the door of any school again. I was going to be an actor (which given my independence and immaturity at the time was on a par with *I am running off to join the circus*). When I met Christ a year later, I went to my first Bible study. Just before heading out the door to the gathering, my mom said to me (for the umpteenth time, bless her), "You really ought to go to college." That night, the leader of the study was teaching on guidance. He said, "Even though you are young adults, God will still use your parents as a source of counsel. For example, maybe they are saying you ought to go to college . . ." You could have heard an audible thud as my jaw hit the floor. I had never before experienced the creative capacity of God to speak into our stories. The next morning I went down to the local community college and registered for classes, which was a really good decision.

Get counsel from a reasonable source, for heaven's sake. The best counselors are those folks who have a few miles of life they've traveled, and who are hooked up into a real relationship with God.

How much of my false self/woundedness is actually fueling this decision (or indecision)?

The more you know yourself, the more this will prove an immensely helpful category. (And please, as Socrates urged, do not live an unexamined life; know yourself.) What are you historically prone to do when it comes to making decisions? If yours is a story filled with indecision, that "confusion" might have nothing to do with clarity and everything to do with fear, or shame, or a wounded heart. A young man afflicted with relational paralysis (he just couldn't commit to the girl he was dating) came to my friend Craig for counsel. They discovered his indecision was rooted in a childhood wound. As a boy, he loved music, but his father shamed him for it. He killed his dream and his desire, and for years afterward he could not discover "what to do with his life." It had nothing to do with clarity; what was needed was healing.

Are you typically driven by a desire to please others? You don't want to choose a grad school, a career, or even a spouse just to make someone else happy. Are you ruled by insecurity? You don't want your false self committing you to a profession simply because it's "safe."

Don't give your false self the keys to the car.

Am I holding back from stepping up?

As a man, this is something I always need to watch out for. Given our core fear of failure—leading the parade of fools, twirling my baton—and given the DNA we got from Adam, who was paralyzed in his moment of greatest trial, I need to be honest with myself and ask, *Is it simply fear that has me "confused" right now?* Confusion is a nice way out of tough decisions. Example: You want to ask a girl out, but you're "not sure." What we usually mean by "not sure" is we aren't sure what she'll say—she might say no. This isn't so much a matter of guidance as it is one of courage. In this case, what's the worst that can happen?

Paralysis (masquerading as "confusion") haunts every man when a looming decision will require a lot of us. Make note of that; don't let it keep you from seeing the light in front of you. God is here to help us with our fears, but only once we name it as fear and do not hide behind, "I just don't know what to do."

What do I sense God saying about this?

You are friends with the brightest person in the universe—have you asked his opinion on the matter? This seems so obvious, but you'd be surprised at the number of Christians who don't ask God or give him more than a day to respond.

Now, learning to hear the voice of God, learning to recognize his counsel, is something we grow into. But my goodness—take the time to cultivate this in your life. Over the course of his journey, Santiago gets better and better at reading the signs, or "omens." Read Dallas Willard's book *Hearing God*, or one I wrote called *Walking with God* (it is a helpful book, and only false modesty would keep me from mentioning it here). Yes, it can be frustrating at times, waiting for his guidance—don't let the boy sabotage this with his impatience. Driving home yesterday, I was angry and impatient with the car in front of me. I made a move to pass, fueled by angry passion; my action nearly caused an accident. Sixty seconds later I looked up and saw a road sign that said Do Not Pass. It had a holy weight to it; I felt busted.

God speaks in all sorts of creative and playful ways. The real issue is, are we willing to listen?

Young men in their twenties are in a season of developing courage. It takes courage to seek God and courage to wait for his reply. Resist the false urgency most decisions present themselves with. Honestly, this will rescue you. Most "urgent" decisions actually aren't; you can almost always buy yourself another day or week to get the clarity you need. Reject false pressure to come to a hasty decision, especially in matters as weighty as college or career or love. Invite God into the process. Give him more than a minute or a day to respond.

These questions were critical for me when it came down to my choice to propose to Susie. It was the biggest decision I had made yet, by a long shot, and with that came the confusion and fear that I might be acting too soon. I couldn't always get a clear answer to all of those categories; sometimes I would hear from God but would doubt what was fueling the pressure of my timing. In the end I knew it wasn't impulsive. Choosing to marry Susie was one of the wisest choices I could make. My friends and family completely supported us, and when I felt God give the green light, I stepped forward into asking for her hand.

I was really honored when you asked Mom and me into that process. I loved the way you approached it with honesty, vulnerability, and strength. In the end after weighing all things, you simply stepped up and played the man. It was beautiful.

In my experience lack of clarity typically comes from one of three reasons: God is wanting to speak to something else (like your story of asking for career guidance but what he wanted to speak to was identity); our false self/woundedness is flaring up (as with an unnamed fear, or paralysis, or insistence on taking one course when all the evidence argues for another); or some sort of spiritual opposition. This becomes especially true the more you are trying to step into your true place in the world—do you really think your enemy plans on letting you just sashay into that?

That last bit rings particularly true. It isn't always the decision making that is the hard part . . . I know too many stories of guys who got counsel and felt like they were stepping into the right path, only to have it all come crumbling around them. Take my friend Jay, for example: he had a really strong passion for music and young kids, and after a year or so of prayer he started a worship ministry that seemed great. Not a month went by before his girlfriend was in a serious accident, his partner bailed for personal reasons, and his music was done. It's like his dream was hit with a sledgehammer—what is with the opposition?

Okay, now we are on to something really vital. Just as we couldn't press into the issues of love and women until we addressed identity, so we cannot go further in decision making until we address the nature of the world you are stepping into. What kind of story do you really believe you have found yourself in?

seven

Fighting for Your Life

*Be self-controlled and alert. Your enemy the devil prowls
around like a roaring lion looking for someone to devour.*

—Saint Peter

During our honeymoon, while Susie and I traveled through
Malaysia and were staying with her brother David, a couple of our
other friends who also happened to be on that half of the planet
flew down to meet us for a few days. We were all thrilled to be in
Georgetown, a UNESCO World Heritage Site, with its beautifully
preserved architecture and thriving multicultural scene. What
we didn't know was that Trevor was not doing well physically. A
couple of days in, after late nights and street food, Trevor was
seriously not doing well; but not wanting to miss out on being
together, he came along to dinner anyway.

We were sitting in a Malaysian food court. It was unlike anything I have ever experienced, completely different than your

mental image of an American mall food court. Hired karaoke singers in purple-sequin vests belted out songs from the stage that acted as a maypole for all the multicolored lights strung around the open-air courtyard. David and I were enjoying another oversized Tiger beer as curry mee and noodle soup were plopped on the table by their respective cooks, who then disappeared into the growing crowd.

My attention was only pulled away from the display around me by the sudden arrival of a friend, and the urgent look on her face. "Trevor needs help," she said, and the distress in her voice forced me to wordlessly follow her through the maze of tables and servers and patrons until we reached what must have been the . . . umm . . . facilities. Inside, surrounded by a group of men, was Trevor. He was lying on his back on the floor of what might have been one of the most fetid bathrooms on the planet, covered in what I hoped was sweat. Within moments I was informed that he passed out and hit his head on the floor with what the onlookers could only describe and re-describe as "a sickening *crack*."

As I knelt down next to him, Trevor slowly regained his consciousness, and I saw his eyes searching around the room trying to piece together what happened. While I continued to pray, Susie explained the situation to him while keeping his head secure. I wish I could say this was the first time Trevor had experienced something like this, but he had spent the better part of the last year wrestling with the damage from another head injury, and this incident only exacerbated his despair. "Why, God?" are the only words he spoke before he looked over at me, and in our eyes the emotions of all our friendship, all his pain, all my fervent prayers for life, passed between us so intensely that I doubt I have experienced many other times something so vital.

Whoa. What an intense moment. I know you all had such high hopes for your time together, and I hate that it happened to Trevor, of all people. After all the things that have come against him, that young man does not need one more reason to doubt God. The fetid restroom, the sickening crack—how awful. But the worst part of the story was not the external pieces, but the internal, the cry that issued forth as he came to: "Why, God?" That is the cry of the failing heart, uttered by many broken hearts in bedrooms, in back alleys, and on battlefields. It is the cry of Jesus upon the cross, the *Eloi*. In it all our pain and all our doubts are forced into two words: *Why, God?*

It is in one sense a beautiful cry, because our hearts are still turning toward God, though perhaps raging against him. Beautiful in that we are still looking for an answer or explanation, and looking in the right direction. Hopes dashed by the intrusion of heartbreak demand some understanding, some reconciliation between what might have been and what came to be. But Trevor's cry also reveals something striking, something glaringly absent from his view of the world. I really don't think I'm making too much of it when I say that it reveals what most people believe—that God is the only other player in our story. "Why, God?" meaning, *Why did you do this*, or at best, *Why didn't you intervene?* A far better cry would have been, "May you be damned forever in hell, Satan!"

Do you really think God threw Trevor on the putrid floor of that Malaysian men's room?

Help me here, Sam—what does your generation do with evil? How do you understand its role in the world, and in stories like this one?

We are certainly aware of evil, and the tangible effect of it is impossible to ignore. Stepping out the front door, you'll find a soldier who lost an arm in Iraq, asking for a buck on the freeway exit. Turning on the TV brings a wash of Sandy Hook Elementary, the attack on 9/11, the History Channel looping the atomic bomb. In Guatemala we watched children digging through a garbage dump the size of Central Park, which also happened to be where they sleep. In Africa the sand has seen so much blood: slave markets, genocide, poaching animals to extinction, revolts, child soldiers, and apartheid. News stations and governments around the world use fear to control populations, but what they don't need to fabricate are the bombings, the hate crimes, the twisted work of butcher doctors, country leaders threatening nuclear destruction while people starve in their homes, suicides sweeping high schools as kids try to escape the cruel world. You can drown in the pain of the world.

Political Science Quarterly published a study recently that claimed belief in end times among Christians was causing a lack of action to end issues related to the environment.[1] I don't want to be part of a "sit back and wait for it all to end" generation, and I know that I am not alone. My heart breaks and righteous rage wells up within me when I hear of young girls being sold into prostitution. We want to salve the wounds of the broken, to see the redemption of creation; we want to stop evil wherever we find it. Superman didn't instill that in me. That one was innate. But I don't think we understand exactly where evil is coming from.

Back in Malaysia, in the moment we found Trevor on the floor, we all began praying, fervently. Right then, at the crux of that moment, the power went out in the whole complex, and we were left in the dark. It felt . . . connected.

My son, listen very carefully now because what I am about to say might be the single most important thing I give you for navigating these coming years:

You were born into a savage war.

All the pain and injustice you described—these are not thousands of random tragedies, millions of isolated occurrences of disappointment or even human corruption. These are the outbreaks of an epic battle. You must understand where this is coming from: there are dark and powerful forces set upon the destruction of the human race. Evil is real. Satan is real. Honestly—I don't know how much more evidence it is going to take to wake a sleeping world.

Every story you have ever loved since you were able to understand stories has had at the center the presence of evil, a villain needing to be vanquished. The reason the world keeps on telling itself those stories is because our story has a villain. Satan is quite real; spiritual warfare is one of the most basic and undeniable aspects of reality. Now yes, yes—mankind is certainly capable of unspeakable horrors. But right there at the beginning, when we lost Paradise, the evil one himself was present, engineering the fall of man so that he could take dominion over the earth. That is why the apostle John warned, "The whole world is under the control of the evil one" (1 John 5:19).

I understand Trevor's cry and have uttered it myself on more than one occasion, but a far more realistic and effective response would have been, "The Lord rebuke you, Satan!" For when we turn a blind eye to the overwhelming evidence for the existence of evil, we will never, ever overcome it—like when you ignore the terrible sound coming from your transmission, hoping it will go away. Really, this might be the single most helpful interpretive lens you will bring to bear on your life: we are at war.

I've spent several decades counseling young men and women in their twenties. Far too often when they hear of something like Trevor's collapse in a stinking bathroom halfway across the world, their reactions tend to be along these lines: "Oh wow—how sad. Gosh, bad things sure seem to happen a lot to him." I'm just a little baffled— with all your keen social consciousness, your profound and detailed awareness of the suffering in this world, and your passion for justice, why doesn't your generation want to face the reality of evil incarnate, meaning the reality of spiritual warfare?

I gotta say that during my four years at a Christian college, I rarely heard anything like this. "Spirituality" kind of fell into one of two categories: either it was something that the charismatics were into or it was blown off completely. I don't mean being spiritual; I mean dealing with a "spiritual realm." Quite frankly, what I remember are a few speakers and professors leaning heavily on the verses that point to something like, "Jesus fights for you, leave it to him."

I think we don't engage in this sort of spirituality because we don't really believe it to be true. We have been taught about and generally understand things like UV rays and the current value of the dollar, which we can't see, but is . . . scientific; whereas the people who do believe that demons are real, to the point of talking about them or praying against them, look like nut jobs, frankly. Spiritual warfare sounds like some sort of Christian conspiracy theory.

Yes—until you try it, until that moment comes when you turn to confront your enemy. Then things begin to change, don't they?

Right—until that happens. When we moved into our first place, Susie started having some intense nightmares, something that isn't common for her. After a couple of nights of this, we figured praying against it couldn't hurt, so we tried it. I felt like an idiot at first, speaking out loud and commanding things to leave. I imagined myself as the blindfolded kid swinging at a piñata. But then the craziest thing happened: she stopped having nightmares.

Exactly. You gave that thing a good, solid whack, and the result was wonderful—no more nightmares. This is enormously practical. We aren't speculating on theological nuances; we are trying to protect those we love, find the guidance we need, fight for our dreams, bring some genuine relief to the suffering in this world. Not only does Christianity provide the clearest and truest explanation for evil, it also provides us with weapons to fight it and see genuine results. This was absolutely central to Jesus' worldview. He neither obsessed over the presence of an enemy nor did he ignore it; he directly dealt with it when he needed to and then moved on.

> In the synagogue there was a man possessed by a demon, an evil spirit. He cried out at the top of his voice, "Ha! What do you want with us, Jesus of Nazareth? Have you come to destroy us? I know who you are—the Holy One of God!"
>
> "Be quiet!" Jesus said sternly. "Come out of him!" (Luke 4:33–35)

> Jesus was driving out a demon that was mute. When the demon left, the man who had been mute spoke, and the crowd was amazed. (Luke 11:14)

If I drive out demons by the Spirit of God, then the kingdom
of God has come upon you. (Matt. 12:28)

The disciples followed his example:

The seventy-two returned with joy and said, "Lord, even the demons
submit to us in your name." (Luke 10:17)

Paul practiced it:

Once when we were going to the place of prayer, we were met by
a slave girl who had a spirit by which she predicted the future. She
earned a great deal of money for her owners by fortune-telling.
This girl followed Paul and the rest of us, shouting, "These men
are servants of the Most High God, who are telling you the way
to be saved." She kept this up for many days. Finally Paul became
so troubled that he turned around and said to the spirit, "In the
name of Jesus Christ I command you to come out of her!" At that
moment the spirit left her. (Acts 16:16–18)

The early church fathers practiced it. Really, spiritual warfare has
been accepted as normative in every age and country except where the
arrogant naïveté of the Enlightenment brought its cloud of unbelief—
disguised as "science" or "reason"—explaining away the spiritual
realm. This isn't weird hocus-pocus; this is necessary when you live
in a savage war.

But let's come at this from another angle—why did God make
you and every single man who came before you a warrior? It is a fascinating question, and one that deserves a thoughtful answer. Why do
little boys understand without even being told that they must take up

arms? Swords and spears, lightsabers, superhero powers are a natural part of a boy's imaginary arsenal. Why are the favorite video games of young men games of battle, war, epic conflict? The warrior is so deep in the soul of man you cannot understand yourself as a man without it. Why? God gave us the faculty of love because we are meant to love; he gave us curiosity because we are meant to explore and discover; he gave us the capacity of laughter because we are created for joy. So why the warrior, in every boy and man, from the dawn of time?

It really is not a stretch to suggest that perhaps the reason is because we were born into an epic war, and in his kindness God prepared us beforehand to engage it.

Time for a confession: I love *Halo*, always have, and probably always will in some respect. I don't play anymore, largely out of a choice to get up off the couch and engage in real life, but when I was younger, it was the bonding force of many a friendship and many a rivalry.

Recently I was thinking back on the success and the love so many young men felt for the franchise (the original grossed around $6.43 million[2]). There are plenty of other "first-person shooter" games, yes; the graphics and physics of the game were great but not earth-shattering for the time. So what was it? What about that particular game drew so many of us in? These days, I'm putting my money on the story. Take out most of the details and here's what you are left with: you are an elite warrior, battling what feels like an endless horde, while exploring the monoliths of the Forerunners, a vanished race that you are somehow connected to, and all of mankind depends on you.

If you told me that this life we are living, the reality that surrounds us, was so epic, so urgent, so mythic, I don't know what could make me happier. There was something to the story that struck a chord in so many of us. We want to be needed, powerful, and central even. Add another layer, to walk where some great ancestor, unknown and mythic, laid stone and story . . . oh man. Count me in. I long for such a story to exist and for such a role to be mine.

Consider happiness yours and count yourself in, my son, because that is *exactly* what is true. You are an elite warrior and all mankind depends on you.

The epic urgency you have just described—the world depicted mythically in *Halo* and a thousand other legends—is precisely our situation. (Again—why does your heart long for that? Why would God put such deep ache in the heart of men if there were no corresponding reality which that heart is needed to rise to?) All you need to do is look at the devastation of the world, and you get some inkling of just how vast, brutal, and urgent this battle really is.

Your dreams are opposed; your love is opposed; your life is opposed. Finding your place is opposed; breaking through the barriers is opposed; things as simple as a date and momentous as a friendship are opposed. Let the warrior arise! Learn to fight this stuff, not only for yourself but on behalf of others. The world is a little short on courageous warriors right now.

And let me quickly add, it is not enough that you acknowledge the war. I recently met with a pastor, a good man, who had done much to fight for his life and his calling. He told me he has a sword on his office wall, "To remind me of the battle." But as we spoke of the reality of warfare, it became clear he wasn't actually, really, truly *dealing* with it. He acknowledged its existence but didn't take it any further. A bit like saying, "I know my house is being broken into on a regular basis—sometimes even when I'm home—but I'm not going to do anything about it; I'll just take my chances." It made me think of that brilliant scene in the movie *The Two Towers*, where even though Rohan has been invaded by marauding hoards, the king still will not go out to fight. Gandalf urges him, "You must fight," to which Théoden replies, "I will not risk open war." Aragorn steps in bluntly: "Open war is upon you, whether you would risk it or not."[3]

Open war is upon us, whether we would risk it, or believe it, or adjust our worldview to accommodate it or not. If you had ignored what was causing Susie's nightmares, they would not have gone away on their own. She would still be having them.

A man faces many forks in the road as he journeys through his life—each choice determining what kind of life he is going to live. Will he sell out for money? Will he pursue the girl—and having won her, will he continue to fight for their relationship? Will he risk for his dreams or succumb to fear and resignation? Will he let his health go? Will he fight for friendships? But this one—Will he face evil? Will he become the warrior?—this one will have dramatic repercussions for the rest of his life, because everything else he wants in life he will have to fight for.

This is the fork in the road that divides the men from the boys, whatever their ages might be.

In fact, I have hope that your generation will be the one to finally deal with this on a global scale. Yours is the generation raised on *Halo* and *Call of Duty*—all those video games that so clearly portray a world at war, great evil powers that must be fought. While a number of church leaders with tight underwear wrote essays denouncing those games, I found myself wondering—perhaps this was God's way of preparing you to understand and accept the reality all around you.

But let me ask: How would you live differently if life was as epic, mythic, and urgent as *Halo*?

I think if I saw myself in an epic story, I would walk with more confidence. Everything would have a place in a larger context: be it training parts of myself that are necessary for survival, or the broken beauty around me, the presence of enemies, even my own future in some respect. If it was all real, all visible and knowable, I think I would suit up and head for the front. At least I hope I would.

I'd love to believe that fighting off spiritual warfare can be more than acting like a crazy person. So how do you do this well, without feeling like an idiot the whole time?

Nobody needs to start shouting and waving a Bible over his head; no one needs to fall on the floor foaming at the mouth. Look at how Jesus did it:

> Next Jesus was taken into the wild by the Spirit for the Test. The Devil was ready to give it. Jesus prepared for the Test by fasting forty days and forty nights. That left him, of course, in a state of extreme hunger, which the Devil took advantage of in the first test: "Since you are God's Son, speak the word that will turn these stones into loaves of bread."
>
> Jesus answered by quoting Deuteronomy: "It takes more than bread to stay alive. It takes a steady stream of words from God's mouth."
>
> For the second test the Devil took him to the Holy City. He

sat him on top of the Temple and said, "Since you are God's Son, jump." The Devil goaded him by quoting Psalm 91: "He has placed you in the care of angels. They will catch you so that you won't so much as stub your toe on a stone."

Jesus countered with another citation from Deuteronomy: "Don't you dare test the Lord your God."

For the third test, the Devil took him to the peak of a huge mountain. He gestured expansively, pointing out all the earth's kingdoms, how glorious they all were. Then he said, "They're yours—lock, stock, and barrel. Just go down on your knees and worship me, and they're yours."

Jesus' refusal was curt: "Beat it, Satan!" He backed his rebuke with a third quotation from Deuteronomy: "Worship the Lord your God, and only him. Serve him with absolute single-heartedness."

The Test was over. The Devil left. (Matt. 4:1–11 MSG)

First there is that wonderful NO! No, I am not giving way to this; no, I am not surrendering my heart to that. NO! That is the warrior rising up; those choices are the very thing that develops the warrior in us. Our enemy is a brilliant liar—the "father of lies" is what Jesus calls him—and he bases his attacks on ancient cunning and personal knowledge of what deceptions will work with us. Our job is to choose not to make an agreement with it, and to break those agreements we already have been making with him.

This morning I was jumped by discouragement. This is going to sound pretty wimpy, but my truck wouldn't start, and it almost took me out because I worked on it for two weeks, finally having to replace the alternator (for $750). I thought I was done being stranded in various places, but this morning I heard that powerless *click-click-click* when I went to start it up. What came next wasn't merely my frustration; the enemy was crouching nearby, like a lion in the grass, waiting to pounce. Discouragement came on so thick and heavy, my heart was sinking before I could even rouse a response. Had I waited for my feelings to change, it might have lasted days, and taken down a lot else with it. "I reject this discouragement, in the name of Jesus." That was the first step—do not give way to it. NO!

Then you see Jesus fight back with the truth—with what he knows to be objectively, immovably true, as given us in Scripture. Ours is an extremely subjective age. (*Subjective*, meaning based on our personal experience and point of view, as opposed to objective, meaning based on immovable truth.) We are so experientially oriented, all it takes is for a feeling to sweep over us, or for something to "seem" true, and we swallow it like a dog swallows the cookie dropped on the floor—without even chewing. This makes us easy picking for the enemy. But a warrior will not be so easily fooled: 1 John 2:14 tells us, "I write to you, young men, because you are strong, and the word of God lives in you, and you have overcome the evil one."

Truth. Jesus fought back with what God his Father has said, and then he commanded the enemy to leave. Back to my battle with discouragement—even though my heart was sinking fast, I still had the choice to give way or fight back. "I bring the cross of Jesus Christ against this," was how I continued. "I reject discouragement and I bring the cross of Jesus Christ against it. I banish this in the name of Jesus." Simple, even mundane, but this is where it happens, in the day-to-day battles, the garden-variety attacks like accusation or shame or fear. At least, this is where we learn to fight it, before the big boys come crashing in.

Back in the chapter on love, I encouraged you to read something on the feminine heart. It would have taken us an entire book to begin to explore that wonderful subject, and we haven't the space here. I urge you the same wisdom again—learn about how warfare works; study some basics on dealing with the enemy (try Neil Anderson's *Victory Over the Darkness* and *The Bondage Breaker*, or *Spiritual Warfare* by Timothy Warner). I'll offer a few more secrets I've learned here, but please don't consider this the end of your warrior training.

Let's come back to decision making, relationships, dreams, and desires, and see what difference dealing with your enemy can make. We paused the previous chapter because you described a couple of scenarios where friends thought they were living well—they sought guidance, looked for wisdom—yet still got hammered. That doesn't need to be the end of the story.

Step one: *Interpretation.* Are you even thinking about how warfare might be at play? Any movement toward life, love, goodness, or freedom *will be* opposed, I guarantee it. Especially those first few steps, because that is where we can so easily lose heart. The enemy will hit us hard to try and stop us in our tracks.

This reminds me of the Threshold Guardians in the Hero's Journey, something that most myths and many modern stories follow. Joseph Campbell noticed a recurring story arc in cultures all across the world that he put forward in his book *The Hero with a Thousand Faces.*[4] Before the hero can really begin his quest, he must choose to go, and once he has made his decision, the Threshold Guardians rise up to stop him. Every story that mimics the Hero's Journey will have something like these, not always a physical battle per se, but always the defining moment that will either prove the hero is meant to continue on or stop the unheroic where they stand. Take, for example, *The Hobbit*: the trolls are a group of guardians that block the way to the quest, as are the mountains that crawl with goblins. In *Star Wars* the stormtroopers kill Luke's aunt and uncle, and he can barely get off the planet without being caught or killed. For Santiago in *The Alchemist*, one Threshold Guardian robs him as soon as he steps foot in Africa; later he faces the fear of the imposing desert.

I think one of our Threshold Guardians, maybe one that is always there, is fear. This thing really does play a large role. Maybe that's why it keeps coming up, our choice between fear and courage. Fear whispers to us that we are making the wrong decision or that life is slipping through our hands while we don't make *any* choices. Fear makes the threshold look like the Wall of China or reminds us that we don't like heights halfway up our ascent. It may not be the only Threshold Guardian, but fear is always one of them.

Another personal one is self-doubt, but it also hit Bilbo, Luke Skywalker, and Santiago. *Can I really do this? Should I bother trying? No one thinks I can . . .* The voice of self-doubt is as crippling as fear and sometimes harder to overcome. It doesn't emanate from spiders or heights or the unknown; it is whispered into our ears and saps our strength, poisoning our resolve, turning us back to safety instead of the adventure and life ahead.

Of course. The purpose of the Threshold Guardians is to prevent you from moving forward. Fear works. Self-doubt works. So does confusion, procrastination, laziness, distraction, crisis, and accusation—a zoo of demonic opposition. There is a way to shut them down. The basic formula is given to us by James, the brother of Jesus (who must have seen his older brother do it many times): "Submit yourselves, then, to God. Resist the devil, and he will flee from you" (James 4:7).

Peter urged us to resist as well, and notice how he described our enemy: "Be self-controlled and alert. Your enemy the devil prowls around like a roaring lion looking for someone to devour. Resist him, standing firm in the faith, because you know that your brothers throughout the world are undergoing the same kind of sufferings" (1 Peter 5:8–9).

First, submit. Consecrate whatever you are pursuing to Jesus; submit it to his rule, bring it under his authority. "I bring this job interview under the authority of Jesus Christ," or, "I bring this trip under the rule of Jesus Christ." Or even a date, and especially a relationship. "I bring this relationship under the rule of Jesus Christ and under his authority. I proclaim Jesus Christ the Lord of this." When we bring our concerns under the rule of Jesus Christ and his authority, it gets them under his protection and provision. You'll want to pray this specifically and repeatedly. This one choice will do a lot to prevent the thief from getting in and fouling things up.

Step two: resist. Bring the work of Christ against every attack as specifically as you can. Let's say you are trying to start your own company or lead a team overseas, and everything keeps unraveling. Here's what I would pray: "I bring the cross of the Lord Jesus Christ against all sabotage and destruction. By the blood of Jesus Christ, I cut off sabotage and destruction from this project in every form and in every way. I bind all sabotage and destruction from me, from this project, and from this immediate next step (whatever that is)." Practice this and you won't feel like a boy swinging at the piñata; you will begin to feel like an elite warrior.

Or maybe it's guidance and clarity that are not coming through. Don't just give up and take a stab at a decision—fight the opposition! "I bring the cross and blood of the Lord Jesus Christ against all opposition to me hearing from God. I bring this decision-making process back under the rule of Jesus Christ right now; I consecrate my own ability to hear and discern what God is saying to me. Jesus said, 'My sheep listen to my voice' (John 10:27) and he promises, 'Call to me and I will answer you' (Jer. 33:3); and so I break every attempt of my enemy to interfere with my decisions, to cut off or confuse me in any way. I bring the cross and blood of Jesus Christ against all confusion, fog, malaise, doubt, and I bind them from me now in the name of Jesus Christ." Honestly, do that a few times and you'll be amazed at the light that begins to break through.

(Readers—we've included a few prayers at the end of this book to help you learn. The Daily Prayer will surprise you with the level of fog it lifts and the amount of breakthrough it alone will usher in.)

But again, let me pause and ask you, Sam: What have you been learning as you pursue your dreams, especially as it relates to writing this book? Has it gone easily? What have you had to do to get breakthrough?

You know, sometimes it really should be quite obvious, but it isn't always. Often I sit down to write, and this little voice says, *You suck. You are a terrible writer. You can't do this. Just go get a beer already.* I mean, it's a *little voice* for crying out loud . . . you'd think *that* would be obvious! Once I've pushed through those and am able to open up a document, I'll try and spend a couple of hours at the computer. A professor I knew once said, "The greatest tool a writer can have is glue to keep him in his chair." Maybe instead of glue it has been praying, every time, no matter what. If I don't pray, no writing happens. Seriously. So I've learned to first consecrate the book, my office, the day, my gifts, pretty much anything that pops into my mind and feels important and relevant. Then I ask God to guide me and to write through me, to give me the words, and then I write. Sometimes I think God speaks and sometimes I think he doesn't. But to be honest, without the framework of warfare, prayer seems weird, like tai chi or a beauty pageant contestant wishing for world peace. But I do know this: if I didn't pray, this book wouldn't have happened.

Bingo. In fact, all the disciplines of the spiritual life feel stupid and boring until we see them as preparation for the savage war coming against us. Open war *is* upon us and you *are* the warrior fitted for your times. Without this, life is random and disappointing. But with this, life is the very battle every boy has wanted to fight since he was young.

eight

A Few Questions About God

I believe in Christianity as I believe that the sun has risen: not only because I see it, but because by it I see everything else.

—C. S. Lewis

They earned the name "The Gates to Hell," and walking through them that foggy October morning everyone was quiet. The wet air muffled the sound of our footsteps, and our breath could be seen pushing through barbwire fencing and dilapidated wooden buildings as we trudged our way along our tour. I wondered what the others were thinking. Were they paying attention to every word our guide said in case it ended up on a test, or were they lost gazing into the eyes of the photographs lining the wall? One thing I knew for certain: no one can come here and not cry out, *Why?*

I don't know when I slipped into agnosticism on my semester abroad. We traveled across Europe for four months, visiting art galleries and battlefields and museums and churches and national landmarks. It was the trip of a lifetime, and it was brutal. Everywhere we went the voices of history hummed a similar tune, their notes being war and death, corruption of the church and the abuse of kings, nationalism and assimilation, human triumph and the rise of secularism. History is riddled with blood and sin.

In Italy I visited a church that was built on top of a relic of an ancient Roman temple, to which god I don't remember, which in turn had been built on top of an even older pagan holy ground and burial site. The builders just keep slapping on a new level to fit the current religion, like adding a new layer of paint to an old barn. In Istanbul I wandered the ornate hall of the Hagia Sophia, which Constantine's mother built as a church, which later became a mosque, and nowadays is a museum that still has speakers on the roof to amplify the call to prayer five times daily, in a country that forbids public displays of religion in order to comply with their posture of a secular nation (despite the fact that 98 percent of the population is Muslim). And back on that cold morning, I trudged through the remains of Auschwitz, wondering, *Why . . . how . . . what God could allow this?*

Now, not all of the trip was bad, not all of history is wicked. In fact much of those months was filled with beauty and wonder. But after witnessing firsthand the effect of a church that manipulated kings and the kings who invented religion, I couldn't blame the people of Europe for turning to secularism. After wandering the confused halls of cathedrals and the tombs of thousands, I couldn't tell you who God was. But I also couldn't tell you that he didn't exist. There was too much redemption peeking out to deny that.

Then I returned to school and was met with the chaos of Western Christianity. Denominations of every hue and more springing up each week, people calling themselves Christians and committing horrible acts of judgment and cruelty (I'm looking at you, Westboro Baptist), friends claiming they bathed in "glory" and losing themselves in fits of laughter. I found the church so unattractive upon my return. Here it was splitting in every direction; there it was using the right language but practicing like a cult. One crazy person yelling, "Turn or burn!" on the street corner can do more damage for Christianity than a hundred atheists.

I know Augustine said, "Since it is God we are speaking of, you do not understand it. If you could understand it, it would not be God,"[1] but frankly that didn't help me with my questions that were far from answered, and the cumulative effect was to surface some serious doubts. Despite the upbringing I had, or maybe because of it, I feel as though I have wrestled with faith as much as anyone. But I've gotten the impression from a good part of the church that somehow questions are bad, that I just need to "believe." So what do I do with my doubts—just bury them?

Questions are good; God welcomes our questions. He doesn't expect us to believe him or trust him without good reason to do so. Many people can relate to your experience abroad, when some darkness in the world or the "sin and blood" of human history ushered in serious doubts. Sometimes the evening news can take me out. I think most caring people hit a crisis of faith at some point in their lives, usually triggered by a personal tragedy or because their education seemed to undermine any intellectual foundation for their faith. Though we tread humbly into realms that may contain elements of mystery, one of the shining qualities of Christianity is that it provides answers— real, solid answers—and not just dogma or "beauty pageant wishes for world peace."

If you recall the story of doubting Thomas, Jesus didn't ignore his questions. Thomas heard rumors of a risen Christ but needed something more to go on than the experience of his friends; Jesus appeared to him personally, and invited him to see for himself the wounds of his hands and feet. He addressed Thomas's doubts directly—no smoke and mirrors; then he urged him to "stop doubting and believe" (John 20:27). Christian faith is not an act of mental suicide. If you feel like something smells like dog squat, you are not expected to go ahead and step in it. (And there is no squat like religious squat.) Many young people feel backed into a corner: turn a blind eye to the stinking parts of religion out of loyalty to their church or a sincere desire to stay with God, or let the squat foul everything and reject faith altogether. One of the things I love about you, Sam, is your intolerance for anything stinking of BS; your instincts are important—don't ignore them. They will lead you to the real deal.

Maybe a word about doubt and "faith" is appropriate here, before we go on. As a millennial, you have been raised in the culture of postmodernism; no, that's not quite right. You've been gasping for a breath of fresh air in the poison gas of postmodernism. Doubt is now embraced as inevitable, a badge of authenticity. As you witnessed firsthand in Auschwitz, dogmatic and authoritative people have done unspeakable harm in the name of "truth" or "being right." Millennials don't want to be associated with anything smacking of the dogmatic and oppressive, so they embrace doubt as a kind of virtue. Allan Bloom described their conviction like this:

> The true believer is the real danger. The study of history and of culture teaches that all the world was mad in the past; men always thought they were right, and that led to wars, persecutions, slavery, xenophobia, racism and chauvinism. The point is not to correct the mistakes and really be right; rather it is not to think you are right at all.[2]

So doubt has become a sort of refuge—not only from the errors of the past but frankly from the burden of action that clarity requires. Doubt is easy; conviction requires courage. The law of entropy is constantly at work here as well; conviction naturally gives way to skepticism if we do not exercise a kind of tenacity. So, to be clear, doubt is not a virtue. Humility is a virtue, including intellectual humility, but doubt in its current cynical form has nothing noble about it when it abandons the search for answers—like a man lost in a city who simply slumps down onto a park bench and stays there.

In our doubting, postmodern culture, "faith" has come to mean something along the lines of, "choosing to believe in spite of the evidence," or, "personal convictions important to you but irrelevant to the rest of us," or simply, "trying to be positive, holding on to hope." Oprah talks about having faith; nearly every president throws it in his boilerplate campaign speech. It's come to mean almost anything, really. But the Christian position is not "believe anyways," or "believe in spite of all reason." Christianity is *not* a "blind leap of faith" as many have been led to believe. According to Jesus—and the entire canon of Scripture—faith is trust and confidence in a person whom you have good reason to believe is trustworthy. So God welcomes our questions, even our ranting and raging, so long as we are really seeking answers. So fire away with your questions.

Okay, here they are:

It seems like the majority of brilliant people—PhDs and scientists and such—pretty much laugh at Christianity. Even at my Christian college there was an air of, "Christianity is an embarrassment intellectually . . . it's called faith for a reason." Which sure implies that religion really is just "the opiate of the masses" like Marx claimed it to be.[3] The psychiatrist Irvin Yalom thinks we invented it to escape the fear of death, and I wonder if they both are right.[4] Maybe this is why the church keeps on splitting—because we all are reforming Jesus into our personal savior who condones the way we live our lives. It's nice—we get saved and don't need to change anything or feel guilty about buying new stuff every month. Anne Lamott said, "You can safely assume that you've created God in your own image when it turns out that God hates all the same people you do."[5] There certainly is a lot of god-awful stuff claiming to be "Christian."

And what about all these other religions? Is there more than one path to whatever salvation is offered? Some of the kindest people I met were Muslim, and some of the worst were Christian. It can't be that only those with the right label get into the special club, can it? Will everyone have a chance in the end to "know" God? Near the end of the story of *The Last Battle*, when the Calormen "pagan" finds himself in heaven, I love what Aslan said: "'Beloved,' said the Glorious One, 'unless thy desire had been for me thou wouldst not have sought so long and so truly. For all find what they truly seek.'"[6] I love that story, and I want it to be the case—that those who are living a good life are seeking God whether they know it or not. But I know that we can't just wish things to be true—or we would all have lightsabers.

Yes, I love that story too. But let's take your questions carefully, one at a time, or we'll get lost in the woods chasing fireflies. Thoughtful questions deserve thoughtful answers. Let's start with, "Is Christianity an opiate, an intellectual embarrassment, false comfort for the ignorant and unenlightened?"

Majorities aren't exactly a good means of discovering truth. The majority of Americans eat fast food—you wouldn't want to take your dietary cues from that fact. Your generation is quick to sniff out attitudes that are nothing more than cultural conformity, so it would be good to keep in mind that the university is a culture as well, a very strict culture where skepticism and relativism are nearly required for membership. Professors yearn for acceptance and admiration like anyone else (not to mention job security), so there is a lockstep conformity in the academy, one part of which includes dismissal of Christianity—even though most professors have actually never looked into the evidence for themselves.

Yes, many intellectuals and academics dismiss the Christian faith. But then you have to account for the myriad of equally brilliant men and women who have found in science and history reasons *supporting* their faith. For every Bertrand Russell or Stephen Hawking, you have to account for a Pascal, Dostoevsky, or even Einstein (who believed in God). Your average freshman may not know it, but there is nothing even close to an "intellectual consensus" in rejection of Christianity. Come to think of it, there isn't an intellectual consensus on *anything* in the academy nowadays, so that is hardly a defining statement on your faith.

When you take it honestly, open-mindedly, question by question, the intellectual support for *un*belief is about as stable as the stock market. Take the creation of the world—the more we discover about the intricate complexity, harmony, and interdependence of the natural world, the more we realize that to believe this all came about by some sort of cosmic accident stretches belief far beyond the breaking point; it is magical thinking of the most obvious kind, a leap of faith *way* beyond anything Christians are accused of.

Much of what thoughtful people are rejecting when they reject

Christianity is actually the embarrassing parade of Christian *culture*—all the "plastic Jesus" nonsense. It will help you so much to separate Christianity from the carnival of Christian "culture" out there (oh, how I wish the unbeliever could do this, even for a moment!). Big hair, gold thrones, lots of shouting—those are a reflection not on Christianity but on the people who indulge in Vegas-style antics. Music is a great comparison—music in itself is a wonderful gift. But over the years mankind has made some pretty stupid music, some really kitschy music, and some downright heinous music. That doesn't prove music is stupid, kitschy, or heinous—it only proves people can be. But that's nothing new. The same holds true for sex—people can get pretty bizarre with sex, but that doesn't prove sex is bizarre.

There are a lot of embarrassing religious people out there—Christians included. That isn't an argument against Christianity any more than pulp fiction is an argument against literature, or domestic violence an argument against marriage. Do some people find a mindless refuge in religion? Of course they do; they also find it in music, sex, food, exercise, and a host of other good things.

Those who take religion seriously have to examine the truth claims being made. Is there a God? What does he require of us? What happens to us when we die—is the soul immortal, and if so, how do we make sure we are welcomed into heaven? Here is where Christianity is utterly unique among world religions. There was a man named Jesus of Nazareth. He claimed to be the Son of God (Buddha never claimed that; Mohammed never claimed that). He said he came to reveal the true heart of God to us, and to give us a life that would never end (eternal life). Any thoughtful consideration of Christianity has to begin here—not with the Jesus freak but with Jesus himself. If the claims of Jesus of Nazareth are true, the implications are staggering.

Now to the question about how Christianity views other faiths.

In *Mere Christianity* C. S. Lewis explained that Christianity does not expect you to believe that other religions have no truth at all to them. God has set a witness in the heavens and in the conscience of man (Ps. 19; Rom. 1). You see a groping toward truth in other religions, like the first light of dawn. But the fullness of truth is found in Jesus Christ, and as a result of his coming, we have the definitive revelation of God. You have something utterly unique in Jesus Christ. The beautiful thing about the dilemma is that we are not sorting through reams of tedious theological nuance; we are confronted with something disruptively clear and startlingly immediate in the person of Jesus Christ.

Which brings me to maybe the root of my questions: How important is the Bible? If it is a fallible work, inspired by men, with some helpful but not fundamentally truthful teachings, then I don't need to feel guilty about not reading it and, really, it shouldn't play any role in my life. This effectively makes Christianity the biggest conga line of fools in the history of the planet, and the promise of redemption and salvation just a placebo. It's all a sugar pill meant to calm us down as we die from cancer.

Yep. If the Bible is not a trustworthy document, then chuck the rest like bad mayonnaise. If you don't have a reliable Bible bringing you the words of God, you don't have any means to the real Jesus, and you don't have Christianity. You can't reject one and hang on to the other (though I know people try). That's like saying your friend is a pathological liar, but other than that you have a solid relationship.

Again, it is helpful to make clear what is actually being claimed here—the Bible claims to be the reliable Word of God to us and not a creation of man. Actually, it makes a number of staggering claims that are way beyond outrageous—unless of course it *is* the Word of God, in which case he is perfectly entitled to make those claims.

Now here's a funny thing about all the fuss over the Bible—the reliability of the manuscript, the apparent internal contradictions, the tension of translation, and so on. All of that hand-wringing on both sides begins with an extraordinary assumption: that the God who created sunlight, the eye, blue whales, mathematics, and more than 170 billion galaxies cannot take care of his message to us. He somehow lost control over the letter he wrote you, and he can't get it back. Really now, think of it—if you begin with the assumption that God does not exist, then you cannot believe in a Word from God; but if you accept God exists and is capable of sustaining the staggering beauty and complexity of the heavens and the intricate, pulsating diversity of life on this planet, then you have to ask if that kind of God could sustain his intention to communicate through the Bible.

I love Dallas Willard's simple position on the Bible:

On its human side, I assume that it was produced and preserved by competent human beings who were at least as intelligent and devout as we are today. I assume they were quite capable of accurately interpreting their own experience and of objectively presenting what they heard and experienced in the language of their historical community, which we today can understand with due diligence.

On the divine side, I assume that God has been willing and competent to arrange for the Bible, including its record of Jesus, to emerge and be preserved in ways that will secure his purposes for it among human beings worldwide. Those who actually believe in God will be untroubled by this. I assume that he did not and *would not* leave his message to humankind in a form that can only be understood by a handful of late-twentieth-century professional scholars who cannot even agree among themselves on the theories that they assume to determine what the message is.[7]

There is evidence aplenty for the asking. There is more support for the Bible than any other ancient manuscript, and more is added every year (the discovery of the Dead Sea Scrolls being one of the highlights of the twentieth century). On the whole we have good reason to be sure the book we read is the book as it was written. As for the reliability of what is contained in those pages, archaeology and historical inquiry continue to confirm claims in the Bible about the location of places and events. David actually was king over Israel from 1010 to 970 BC; Solomon built the temple and we know precisely where; Jesus of Nazareth lived at the time of Herod Antipas. And the apparent inconsistencies—for example, Matthew said Jesus healed two blind men upon leaving Jericho; Mark said he healed one—do not amount to anything like substantive contradictions in the message. The gospel writers could have easily chosen to report different events, or emphasize portions of those events they considered to be important to their audiences (Matthew wrote to fellow Jews, Mark to the Gentiles).

All this to say, your average man on the street has "heard" that the Bible has long been debunked by science or history when in fact nothing of the sort has happened. They've swallowed their culture's assumptions whole without even giving it a day or two of personal investigation.

I would be guilty of that myself. I think a great deal of the unbelief of my generation is simply assumed as what any thoughtful person should believe. It's a learned posture toward things like mass media and the fine-tuned BS detectors that my generation has sharpened after years of being the subjects of marketing. Things like religion and information have become the sort of topics we take for granted as untrustworthy.

Exactly, which is why one of the great questions of the ages is why so many people continue to regard the Bible at all. After centuries of abuse, neglect, persecution, academic assault, schisms . . . after eons of human suffering, in the face of horrifying corruptions by its alleged ambassadors, the Bible continues to be the most influential book in the world, providing men and women of vastly different cultures and backgrounds a profound connection with God and interpretation of life. How do you account for that? Self-delusion or mass deception simply cannot be sustained on such a scale, and those arguments crumble against the evidence.

Really—if the Bible is only the musings of men *claiming* to speak for God, it is just too badly done to pull it off. It reads far more like a torrid love story than an edict of doctrine or manifesto for a religion. God gets angry, then forgives and weeps, then rants and rages and ends up sounding like a jealous lover; Jesus falls asleep at crucial moments, chooses a ridiculously small and inept group to start a global revolution, then seems to give way to fear and doubt at the climax of his greatest trial. This just isn't the kind of book you would write to convince the masses that Jesus was God or some mythic hero. If the Bible were constructed by men to pose as a divine manuscript, even the sloppiest scribe would have taken out apparent inconsistencies and embarrassing moments. And there is no way they would have included stories like Tamar seducing her father-in-law, David's affair with Bathsheba and murder of her husband, or the embarrassing, petty schisms in the early church. The Bible is too brutally honest to be fake.

When given an open and fair read, the book is simply unparalleled.

Where it speaks to issues of injustice, it is devastating; where it speaks to economics personal and national, it is incriminating; on human suffering its pathos, empathy, and comfort are unequalled; and when it speaks to religion, it is utterly ruthless toward the very BS you and your peers so rightly abhor. At its core the Bible is a book dealing primarily with the human condition and God's remedy for it; on these issues alone it is unrivaled in world literature. Aristotle, Confucius, Nietzsche, Hawking—there is nothing even remotely like it.

If the Bible is true, the implications are huge. I feel as though it would finally lift the curtain that has been weighing on me for some time, the curtain being some kind of film that slows my actions and dulls my faith. For years the Bible was touted as a "life raft" for people—get in or burn forever. But if the Bible can be trusted, there is so much more there. Jesus' life was radical in how he loved, whom he loved, what he gave value and what he didn't. If he was really the God-man, then maybe I can begin to model his drive and passion and not feel like a fool pretending to be a comic book superhero. I digress a little, but it is really exciting.

Maybe my deepest questions got in because of what Auschwitz symbolized—the problem of pain. How can we trust in a good and loving God with all the pain and suffering in the world? I've taken enough theology and philosophy classes to hear several answers to this, so let's refine it a bit. Instead of focusing on the whole "problem of pain," let me instead ask this: Jesus came and died for our sins and ushered in the coming kingdom, right? The language we use is a sort of "now but not yet" kind of stuff. Why, if he has won, does it sometimes seem like he lost? Why do things need to get worse before he . . . what, wins again?

The "problem of pain," of evil in the world, certainly seems like the most compelling argument against a loving and sovereign God. But let me suggest something for consideration. According to Christian belief, God is a God of love and created a world for love. In order for love to be real, you have to allow people to exercise their own free will. Love is meaningless if it is not freely chosen; you want Susie to choose you totally apart from any sort of force or compulsion.

By allowing creatures other than himself to exercise free will—both men and angels—God therefore allowed for the possibility of evil. He did not create it, but he did allow for the possibility. It was first angels, then mankind who chose to allow evil into the story. The Bible is filled with God's hatred of evil, his empathy for our suffering, a myriad of promises that he will comfort and sustain us, that he will intervene—and again, you have the witness of the church down through the ages that he *has* comforted, sustained, and dramatically intervened. Finally, we have Jesus Christ, his stunning answer to our dilemma. Through Jesus, God overthrows all demonic powers and at the same time provides for the cleansing and renewal of the human heart. And that, by the way, is the real dilemma of the earth—how to deal with evil in the human heart. Religion only seems to make it worse. Jesus actually renews our hearts, if we will surrender to him. It is surely his most breathtaking work.

The second question has to do with timing. I'm not qualified to speak to the issue of why God didn't just wrap it all up shortly after the resurrection of Christ. I can say I am grateful, or neither of us would have been included in the coming wonders.

But let me pause; I'm afraid I may have gone on a bit and sounded like the old guy holding forth. Let me ask you, Sam—in your journey toward your own faith convictions, what has proven most helpful, most influential?

I have already hit upon my pragmatism, and the necessary by-product of the "dignity of causation," but they are worth revisiting. Walking through the fields of Europe and the beaches of the West Coast, I made the choice to engage my doubt. Many of my fellow travelers chose *not* to doubt, to blindly press their Bibles to their faces and not wrestle with the questions right in front of us. Likewise back in the comfort of suburban neighborhoods and social majorities, too many young men and women never shift from being spoon-fed their daily dose of faith. Questioning the obvious mysteries, asserting myself as an individual with a unique path to walk, acknowledging the place I have in history and the noble and the wicked choices made by those before me to bring me to where I stand, and then taking all this and talking about it with the men and women I respect . . . that is the *only* way to begin to understand. Thus this book.

I learn by doing more often than I learn by watching others, but part of that doing is the discourse I need to build a framework of the world around me, of who I am and what I believe. If it wasn't for Jon or Justin or Drew or Laurel or Susie or countless others, I might be sailing around the Sea of Cortez muttering to myself like Macbeth, "Life's . . . a tale / Told by an idiot, full of sound and fury / Signifying nothing."[8] But I am not there, and I know now that though I may not always have the answers, choosing to engage the questions with the people around me can bring about the answers I seek.

More than anything else, though, I've found that beauty and goodness root me far beyond theology or orthodoxy or conversations. There came a time after I had returned from Europe that I felt I needed to come off the fence that was my agnosticism. I didn't want to stay in that posture, and immediately all of the times I have experienced staggering beauty in creation and true goodness in people came rushing to mind. I can't believe that all of that is without meaning. It is too powerful. So I got off the fence, not out of a fear of death and what comes after, not because of some radical sermon, but because beauty is genuine, goodness is genuine, and it must come from somewhere.

So how do we continue to learn where and who this comes from? Is there a genuine, authentic relationship to be had with God? The take on this seems to be as diverse as the denominations out there: I've got friends who are diving in to the church thing, some friends who have their daily "quiet time," another who goes to every charismatic conference, and a few who will go surfing or hiking to be with God (something I found myself doing . . . nature has always made me feel closer to the Creator, but often I'd find myself singing Katy Perry to myself instead of trying to talk to God). So, how do you cultivate a genuine spiritual life? Blanket question. More specifically, are there some things we should do that might not come easy to build a relationship with God, or can we find him in whatever we prefer to do on our own and he will "meet us there"?

Again, because we live in such a subjective climate, where "spirituality" can mean anything, let's be clear on what it is we want to cultivate. The Christian faith is at its center an invitation to intimacy with God. He is an actual person, with a personality and a heart just like you, and just as in any other relationship, it is the connection of these two hearts that matters above all else. This is where we separate from religion, and this is what will rescue us from slipping back into it. Friendship with God is the heartbeat of it all; nothing else can substitute (though many things will try).

So, the question is, how do you cultivate friendship and intimacy with God? (Isn't that more refreshing than, "How do I get more serious about my religion?") Simply ask yourself, "What would I do to cultivate a deeper intimacy with Susie, or with any of my friends?" Time together, talking about life, processing both your inner and outer experiences—it seems painfully obvious but it honestly is that simple. So let's pause for a moment and give space to God in our hearts:

> *Jesus, I need you. I need your love and beauty and life. I need your grace for all my shortcomings, and I need your beautiful strength to live as I was meant to live. I open my heart to you; I give my life to you. Come and live in me. Draw near to me. Restore me in your love. I surrender my life to be yours forever.*

And always, always, always remember *we are at war.* You have an enemy; his attacks are the primary reason most people can't "connect" with God. It's not them; it's not God. It is usually some sort of fog, accusation, dullness, or spiritual interference the enemy has brought in. Don't forget this—just as you will need to fight for your relationship with Susie, you will need the warrior to rise up for your friendship with God.

I was reading Athanasius' *Letter to Marcellinus* the other day (older guy writing to younger guy, just like this) and this phrase leapt off the page: "You are successfully enduring the present trial, although you have suffered many tribulations in it, and you have not neglected the discipline."[9] Down through the ages the spiritual disciplines were seen as a way of strengthening the warrior in us, to win the battles before us. Certain practices have proven helpful—such as silence and solitude (which rescue you from your culture's constant demands). Certainly worship and the sacraments. Good teaching. You have the Scriptures as a beginning point (and they continually rescue us from our subjective spirals). But only as part of an organic whole that includes those things particular to your friendship with God—walking on the beach, reading a great book, listening to music, dinner, and laughter with friends.

Augustine said, "Our hearts are restless until they find their rest in you."[10] The heart is essential for knowing God; the heart is the means. Therefore, the more awake and aware, the more healed and available your heart is, the more you will find you can connect with God. Pay attention to the life of your heart—where are you looking for love, or meaning, or comfort, or identity? Take that to God; invite him right there. Where are you anxious, or angry, or lonely, or filled with joy and playfulness and yearning for adventure? Invite God there.

Hang out with people who know and love God—they should be the core of your circle of friends. But you can also enjoy their "company" through books and by attending their talks. Remember—we aren't talking about a nice little addition to our lives; we are in a vicious battle for our hearts and everything we love. We cannot hope to win without God—*that* is the context for seeking him, for cultivating a "spiritual life." This is life and death, not another round of "Amazing Grace."

I just want to come back to the implied excitement of this! I know that for many of us religious language can feel stodgy and recycled, but when you speak of the heart, and of drawing closer to God through people and what you love, of fighting for it like any relationship, the ideas are not recycled, and the results promise a refreshing and exciting outcome. One of the books that helped me recover faith was Chesterton's *Orthodoxy*, where he said, "People have fallen into a foolish habit of speaking of orthodoxy as something heavy, humdrum and safe. There never was anything so perilous or so exciting as orthodoxy."[11] I love that. My hope has been to have a genuine relationship with God, and with others, to come together as a church (lower case) and explore what he is saying, and to walk strongly with a solid foundation. It is a thrilling promise.

nine

The Collision of Intimacy

There are only three things to be done with a woman. You can love her, suffer for her, or turn her into literature.

—Lawrence Durrell

It's been a long day. I have been running around town doing odd errands that needed tending to, I wrote for a few hours before that, and when Susie got off work, we went to the climbing gym before making dinner. I am dog-tired, and so relieved to be falling into bed. But before I can turn off the light, Susie has rolled over on her side, let out quite the sigh, and begun to rehash the day through what seems to be an unending flow of questions and conversation. *You're kidding me*, I think to myself, *doesn't she know beds are for sleeping?!* The answer is no, she does not. I do have the escape of controlling the one light, which she knows signals my imminent slumber once turned off. When we moved into the guest room at the ranch this summer, which has two lights, her face was that of pure twisted pleasure when she looked at me and left her light on, and I knew I was trapped.

I have said this before, but as the saying goes it bears repeating: Susie and I are opposites in so very many ways. We clearly approach sleep differently. She wakes up much like a puppy, all bright eyed and excited to be in a new day, while I am what you might call . . . slow to rise. I don't see what's so great about this new day and why it has robbed me of the joy of dreamland. I run at a steady pace, fit for one that has chosen other things for the past twenty years, that is to say, not always the essence of elegance or speed. Susie runs like the soundtrack to *Chariots of Fire* is audible, and I believe I once saw a gazelle take notes to improve its grace and form. She treats every new acquaintance as a best friend, while I have adopted the old judiciary model of "guilty until proven innocent" and wait for the person to win my favor. When Susie is with me, we eat quite well, whereas once I am left to my own devices, I dine on Korean Ramen. Ironically, I like nice things and she can live without them quite happily, whereas she pines over good cheese and I am lactose intolerant.

Now, add to this the reality that she is always there. ("Duh, Sam. What did you expect?") Okay. So it doesn't sound profound, but let me continue. Having Susie around, living with her, exploring life together, has been a tremendous joy and is a key part of marriage, but what I didn't expect was how that feels sometimes. Someone once described marriage as though a mirror has moved into your life, but I think it's more than that. Let's add that this mirror is following you around all the time and can talk like the teapot from *Beauty and the Beast*, and then I think you begin to get the idea. All of the good things about myself are constantly reflected back at me, which also means that all of my failures and deficiencies get their turn in the spotlight.

Before Susie, I could be out with my friends and be in a foul mood, and I would be able to dismiss it to them all as just that, a mood. I could apologize for being angry or checked out or grumpy, and then go back into isolation. Everyone only saw glimpses of me, hours at a time, but that was before. Susie knows who I am when I am in public, and who I am at home. The dilemma is obvious: all of my issues, my inadequacies, my failures, become this siren blaring out that neither of us can ignore. It's amazing . . . I want to get angry with her for exposing me, and then I want to pull away and hide somehow, to disengage. I found myself thinking the other day after she raised her eyebrows in response to some rude comment I made about a friend, *Leave me alone! Let me be broken for five minutes!*

Yep. Yep. Yep. You have plunged into the glorious encounter with the Other. It is one of the greatest gifts of our existence, and by far the most radically disruptive. It's startling, really. The "otherness" of gender is particularly disruptive in especially wonderful ways. I can be cruising along fine through my day, and then Mom walks into the room and simply her presence is like someone turning on the stereo; sometimes it's Beethoven and sometimes Twisted Sister, but I have to *pay attention* and that is really, really good for me.

We were visiting some friends in Hawaii back in January. They took us out sailing in hopes of seeing dolphins, maybe even humpback whales. (The whales migrate there in winter to calve and breed in the warm waters—fabulous idea, isn't it?) As we came upon the whales, our friends invited us to don snorkel gear, get in the water, and swim toward them—an invitation that was at once thrilling and pretty deeply unnerving. We were far from the coast; whales are massive creatures, and they aren't the only huge things swimming around out here. As we cautiously kicked along we first encountered a mother and her calf, then a single adult humpback that was simply hovering in the water not far below the surface. We held our breath and dove down . . . and got really close. I was maybe twenty feet from a creature that weighed fifty thousand pounds and ran forty-five feet long.

Then I saw its massive eye, about the size of a salad plate. It was looking at me.

Back on dry land it took me a good hour to recover, to try and find words to describe the experience. The best I could do was to say it must be something like when an angel steps into the room and you see him and he sees you. Holy, beautiful, and totally disarming. This is the encounter with the Other, and marriage might be our most intimate, ongoing experience of it.

Sartre felt that "hell is other people,"[1] but precisely the opposite is true—hell is being left alone forever, with no other reality than your own consciousness of yourself. It is being locked in a casket of your own internal chaos with no hope of a window or door letting in light from outside to give you a moment's respite from yourself. Hell is the refusal of the gift of the Other.

The adolescent views the Other as merely an opportunity to gain a sense of self: *the Other is here for me.* He is mainly concerned with what the Other thinks of him, how she treats him, and especially how she doesn't treat him. But as we step into a more mature, loving relationship, we realize the Other is here to call us out of ourselves, beyond ourselves. The first years of marriage can really knock you for a loop in this regard. Opposites really and truly attract—not only in gender, personality, habits, and lifestyle but also *in our brokenness.*

Domineering men typically marry mousy women; domineering women typically choose milk-toast men. Perfectionists often marry someone with massive guilt issues; obsessive-compulsive types marry chaotic spouses. God is in that, by the way—he is using the absolute otherness of your mate to get to the brokenness in you, so that he might heal it. I'm told the only unfinished sentence in the Bible comes at the fall of man. After the betrayal, when Adam and Eve have allowed evil to take dominion, God then said, "He must not be allowed to . . . live forever" almost with a shudder (Gen. 3:22). Too horrifying to think of fallen humanity growing worse and worse with no end in sight.

God is fiercely committed to our transformation; he simply will not allow us to carry on unchanged, and so in his love he gives us . . . our opposite. Crazy-making though it might be, marriage is wonderfully redemptive. But yes, marriage is a massive adjustment, so be kind to your marriage, especially in those first years of getting your sea legs. Recognize that you are both beautiful and broken people in need of restoration.

One expression of kindness to the marriage and to your brokenness is that you've got to take it in doses. You both need some space. Not as a flight from love, but simply because you cannot sustain the constancy of it without some sort of respite. Daily, take a walk, go for a run, read by yourself. Monthly, get away for something you love to do—riding your bike, seeing a movie. Annually, Mom and I try to take a personal retreat, a weekend just to ourselves. Breathing room does wonders for the marriage.

Having said that, one of the greatest expressions of courage will be to move toward Susie when she is not doing well. Just last night, Stasi and I went out for groceries and a quick bite, and man it was hard. She was PMSing and I don't know what else was going on, but it was not enjoyable to be together. I wanted to leave, just get home so I could go be by myself—do you see the flight from the Other? The flight back into your own private sanctuary?

If I have learned anything in these short months, and it is possible that I haven't, I have been made very aware of how often I feel like I cannot fill her. Man, was this discouraging for the two of us. Her relational need can feel simultaneously foreign and larger than my own, like the conversations at night or her ability to befriend anyone. There comes a point where I am content to have no one else around, which occasionally collides with Susie filling our social calendar.

Susie's relational capacity is beautiful. The trouble came when I felt that it was my responsibility to be all she needed. This kicked in right after we got married, and I think it came from a good place—wanting to provide and protect and all that—but the fact is it isn't my role to be everything and everyone to her. When I tried to be all the relational connection she needed, I felt like a failure, which turned out to be a double-edged sword; for when I try to do something for Susie but don't succeed (for whatever reason), she blames herself.

On the one hand she felt bad that I couldn't be enough, *and* she felt like her need was overwhelming. I felt like crap because I couldn't fill her, and I learned that no matter how much I tried, I couldn't make a dent, so eventually I just stopped trying. Why do something if I can't succeed? It's a recipe for feeling like a failure, which I'd like to take a pass on, thank you very much.

This relational capacity of hers began to feel like a source of shame, for the both of us. It was never something she asked me to fill; I just innately (and probably naively) felt that I should fill her every need.

You have stumbled into one of the great mysteries of Eve—she is both a fountain of life and at the very same time a bottomless well. How the two coexist in the same soul I have no idea. But so it is. And there need be no shame. Wonderful as your love may be, she needs a larger relational world than you.

Anytime we moved to a new city, one of my first priorities was to help Mom develop connections with other women. When you boys were young, she had groups like MOPS and Moms in Touch. I'm no fool—she has a relational chasm inside her, and I know we are both going to have a far better chance at happiness if she has a larger circle of connection beyond me. A guy seems to be pretty content all weekend with the game and a cold one, or a book and a bag of chips. Not women, not for the most part. Be a cheerleader of her friendships. In thirty years of marriage I have never once said no when Mom asked if she could go see a movie with a friend, or even spend a girls weekend away.

I cannot fill her goes down as one of the five things I wish I'd known in our first few years, followed by . . .

Get a budget and stick to it. Money really is the major source of marital tension. I thought Stasi's mother was so over-the-hill lame whenever she would say, "Love flies out the window when there's no pork chop on the table." But, Jane, you were right—that was my twenties' "I know everything" arrogance dismissing you.

There's a lot of little girl in there. Surely you have encountered this. When I say things that sound like her father is speaking to her, it is not going to go well. (Which brings us back to "know her story"!) Are you encountering the woman right now or the little girl?

Conflict means something totally different to each of us. It's not just that we handle conflict in completely opposite ways; conflict itself carries a completely different meaning and experience for each of us. What is yours? What is hers? Let hers be the guiding mood so that you don't just blunder in, setting off land mines.

Time means everything. There's just no shortcut to a good marriage. I wish I'd have protected our time together more in the early days. I just did what I wanted, lived like I did before marriage. I didn't sacrifice my plans; I sacrificed the marriage *for* my plans.

You know, I was really good at thinking only about myself pre-marriage, but sacrificing for the Other really has become a joy. If you had told me that a couple of years ago, I might have rolled my eyes at you. It seems to be something I could only learn through experience, kind of the rule for marriage thus far.

Susie has been looking at grad school for a while now, and her program will require all of her time, which means I would need to be working to support both of us. This actually got me really excited. I know it would be a sacrifice of my time to work more while Susie pursues the education she needs to reach her dream, but it doesn't feel like wasted time to me. I need purpose in my work, and supporting both of us for a couple of years would put work into a larger context. Another example that comes to mind is church. I don't always feel the strongest pull to go every Sunday morning (how's that for political phrasing?), but I know Susie really loves it. So we go. And the joy she feels after having been is something I get to share in. By sacrificing my wants for hers, I experience the joy of doing something for her, not to mention how happy she is when she gets to go.

Choosing to sacrifice for her sake has become a love language in its own way. I want the best for Susie, and sometimes the best isn't something I would have chosen were I single. But man, loving her by laying down something of my own and seeing her light up (especially if she doesn't know it was a sacrifice) is one of the greatest joys there is.

Intimacy in marriage has been so rich—especially physical intimacy—but it feels like new frontier. Help me understand some of the wildness.

Most of what needs to be learned here has to be learned through discovery. Just a couple thoughts for now . . .

Humpback whales have been studied more than the common cold, yet no one has ever observed them making love. Once courting has reached a climax, the pair dive deep into the unknown and have their tryst in private. I love that. It speaks of the deep mystery and wild Otherness of sex—something no movie has ever been able to capture. Guys, there's barnyard sex and there's deep-sea diving. Barnyard sex is loads of fun, but it won't cultivate the intimacy you want over a lifetime. As my friend Morgan says, the two big things he's learned in marriage are that for a woman, "money isn't money and sex isn't sex." For a woman money is all about security, while for men it is mostly about adequacy. For a woman, sex is all about intimacy. Women are aroused by words, while men are aroused visually. For sex to dive in to the deep, it has to be about the culmination of a growing soul-to-soul intimacy between the two of you.

(Can you see now that masturbation is the ultimate rejection of the Other? *I don't need you. I don't have to engage you at all.*)

It's all about intimacy. If things feel awkward in the bedroom, it rarely has to do with mechanics. Something is typically wrong elsewhere in the relationship; the soul-to-soul connection has been strained or broken. Ask her how she's doing. Ask her how she thinks the two of you are doing. Talk about your sex life with gentleness. "Do you feel beautiful, honey? Because you are absolutely beautiful to me." "What do you enjoy? Where are we at our best?" Use your words to assuage her fears. Oh man—the intimacy of that conversation will have the two of you ripping each other's clothes off.

And by all means—pray for your sexual joy! God gave us sex (which really ought to put to rest once and for all every doubt about his goodness). He is *for* your sexual happiness, so pray for your sex life. Invite the passionate love of God and the wildness of his Spirit into your communion.

Prayer brings me to one last thought—healing past brokenness. More than anything else, this tends to be what introduces trouble into the marriage bed.

(Readers—You will want to pray through your sexual history— probably first by yourself, though the day may come when you are solid enough in your marriage to pray for each other here. The prayer we've included at the back of the book will prove very helpful in healing sexual history.)

Living with Eve can be really good; in fact living with Susie has been the best part of my life thus far. Yes, there is confusion, and plenty of unknowns, and enough occasional flailing on my part to pass the time. But that doesn't come close to defining us.

We have had a very busy couple of days recently. Three days ago we got up at 3:00 a.m. to meet some friends and climb one of Colorado's 14ers; the next day we drove six hours to be part of a wedding celebration with some dear friends of ours, which we then drove back from the next morning. We leave for a weeklong trip tomorrow. But last night, after driving all day, we went for a bike ride once the sun was going down and the day was cooler. It was beautiful. We rode along a bike path and then cut down by some train tracks to get to a path that follows a stream I had discovered earlier. We talked about loving our time here in Colorado, about our little apartment, about making meals together. As we rode along, I noticed the sky growing dark and threatening to rain, but we were enjoying ourselves too much to cut it short, so we continued to explore the trail. I loved seeing Susie's joy at the beauty of it all. At the moment we started heading home, the rain came, and it came fast.

So we took shelter in the first thing we could find, which happened to be a railway underpass. We probably stood there for forty minutes, first watching the rain, then listening to the train passing overhead, and then pointing out the arcs and veins of lightning crossing the sky. We talked about what kind of parents we want to be, what sort of home we want to create, and how happy we were to be stuck in a thunderstorm. I loved every minute of it.

Marriage has felt like so many moments stolen from time. Like that night under the bridge in the rain, it can seem like nothing else exists and that we have finally stopped the flow of time and seized the present moment. There is nothing else like it. Susie and I have often said that marriage is like having a buddy with you, someone who will adventure and suffer and explore and live by your side. Having Susie by mine has opened more doors than it ever closed, our dreams have changed into new and greater ones, and we continue to change as people—the both of us working on the other. But among all those wonders, it continues to be the small yet timeless moments that we treasure the most. It is amazing how much joy could be packed into so little a thing as that instant, standing close together in the rain.

ten

Racing Toward the Unknown

The true philosophy is concerned with the instant. Will a
man take this road or that?—that is the only thing to think
about, if you enjoy thinking. The æons are easy enough to
think about, any one can think about them. The instant is
really awful: and it is because our religion has intensely
felt the instant, that it has in literature dealt much with
battle and in theology dealt much with hell. It is full of
danger, like a boy's book: it is at an immortal crisis.

—G. K. Chesterton, *Orthodoxy*

The U-Haul is packed. We are heading east, to Minnesota. Susie
got accepted to that graduate program in nursing. I will be co-
creating an online magazine for young men called andsonsmagazine
.com and looking for more lucrative work to support us. We will
live in Minneapolis for three to five years, depending on which
track Susie chooses to follow in her program. For Susie this

means going home, someplace she has not been for years, so it is not hard to guess where the spring in her step comes from. I have been packing our few possessions that, for the most part, were all gift wrapped only a few months ago. We are going to the land of ten thousand lakes and helicopter-size mosquitoes; cheese (I have never seen people eat so much cheese . . . but then I guess I have never been to Wisconsin); hot dishes (I've been told many times that calling it a "casserole" is just getting uppity); and the Vikings (a team that has never won a Super Bowl, but has some of the most dedicated fans; my wife still hasn't forgiven them for signing Brett Favre). It snows on average forty-nine inches per year in the Twin Cities; the high temp in January is 26 degrees, but nonetheless people stand outside and "catch up" for hours at a time.

All these months we have spent diving deeper in to the spoken and unspoken challenges facing us young men (and really all men) feel a bit like suiting up. I have the image in my head of the *Band of Brothers* HBO series, specifically the scene where the men are on the tarmac strapping on ammunition, reviewing maps and objective orders, stripping and assembling their rifles, all waiting to board the C-47s that will drop them over Normandy.

I wonder to myself as I sit on the curb: Have I killed a lion? Right now I feel an uneasiness creeping up and a voice inside that wonders if I would know a lion when I saw one. Maybe that's how this feels. It would sure seem more obvious if I had a lion skin to don like Hercules . . . I'm sitting here on the concrete, and the memories come trickling in.

I was thirteen. The sun was just up above the Wyoming horizon, the crisp alpine air stinging my lungs, gloves three sizes too big blocking my adolescent fingers from grabbing the lip of an overhang on the Grand Teton. Below me was a three-thousand-foot drop to a glacier that stubbornly clung to the rock in the July sun. You sat above me, on a shelf four feet wide, a rope wrapped around your waist that you reeled in as I climbed. Above us, another two thousand feet of climbing before we reached the summit. We trained for that day, and it was an intentional act of initiation into young manhood, one that I remember well twelve years later. Summiting the Grand—boy, was that a lion.

Then there was stepping off into college, a few states away from my family and everyone I knew. Those years were a series of challenges, some inevitable, some chosen. None more impactful than stepping up to apply to be a resident assistant. I felt suited for the task but knew that my reputation would probably inhibit my acceptance. Instead, I was welcomed and affirmed (many times as doubt crept back in) by Jon Young, who would act as a "permission giver" to me over the course of that year. The permission I needed was to be real, despite the voices telling me not to. Choosing to engage, or not engage, the young men of my section was a battle every day. Heck, sometimes just leaving my room was a challenge. I had to face isolation, self-deprecation, the role of mentor, the role of psychiatrist, the role of judge, and every so often, the role of friend. The relationships that last even now are a testament to the many lions that were killed that year.

I ran a half marathon. Me. Me who quit track after two years in high school, who needed to quit smoking to get past the three-mile mark, who had never run more than two miles at a time to begin with. At first it was brutal, and I begged for a smoke mid-run. But then something in me rose to the challenge. I started running five days a week, stopped smoking (mostly), cut down on some of the happy hours (coincidently, this was also the time Susie was entering my life . . .). Now, the race wasn't pretty. As a matter of fact, it wasn't even a registered race, just a group of friends who mapped out a course for ourselves and ran one afternoon; but that didn't matter for my heart. What mattered was that I ran 13.1 miles one sunny day in March, with a group of friends, after a couple months of training, and I never would have guessed I could have.

My junior year of high school we built that Baja Bug together. With the help of a Sawzall and an air-cooled restoration mechanic, we transformed what had been an unobtrusive little '68 Beetle into a beauty that got more second looks than Sofía Vergara. That car was a lady-killer. It was a joy to drive around town, and probably took some years off my hearing. Like most custom cars it also needed constant love and quality time, a toll that I quickly grew tired of paying, but because of the sentimental value of the car, I held on to it for about nine years. The lion came when I needed to sell it. I was getting married, and after the car died on my fiancée a few times, leaving Susie stranded around town, I knew a more reliable means of transport was in order. So I sold it and bought something that should last me another decade (without leaving my lady up a creek). It was hard to say good-bye. I mean, really. But it was a choice to leave some of my boyhood behind and make a responsible decision, which now gives me the peace of mind that I *can* do such a thing.

Stepping up to marry Susie and fighting for our wedding has to count. I felt as though the brief six months of engagement (well, at least now they feel brief) was a time to better myself before that day. It's funny, but somehow I feel as though it is easier for me to push myself when there is an end in sight. Running every day, working on being more gracious, praying more often, choosing to step up and play the man—they were all easier to do when I had an "end date" in mind. As though when I got married, I would either be so used to doing those things that it would come naturally, or they wouldn't matter anymore and I could revert to my old self-centered ways. Oh, how long must I look back at myself and shake my head? Still, as little as I knew, I was aware at least of what I was stepping into, and that I had much to learn, and that it would be tough, the hardest thing I may ever do, but also the most beautiful. That was a lion I knew was a lion. It didn't wait to show its true colors until after the fact; it was one of the few that charged straight in, and conquering it was making the choice to step up and play the man even when there is no end date in sight.

Writing this book has definitely been a lion. This has not been easy, every day fighting off feelings of inadequacy, discouragement, the feeling that I am a fake, pulling off a shtick, not putting anything new or helpful on paper. Choosing to fight what Steven Pressfield calls "Resistance" in his book *The War of Art*, by sitting down and pushing through the lies in order to write. But two words have been taped to my computer as reminders: "poet" for the moments of inspiration, and "warrior" for all the times without. There is nothing quite like putting yourself out there on the page, but this has been a lion I have been excited to tackle.

And tackle it you have. Those are all legitimate lions, every one. You have a right to feel strong. The development of soul-strength takes place subtly, over time—just like physical strength and endurance. Each of those challenges you rose to was more than an event, a moment of victory; a genuine courage and true masculine strength were being formed in you, growing in you each time. More has happened within you than you probably feel, Sam. Remember your bachelor party— that night on the beach, tucked under the cliff around a campfire with your brothers and friends gathered 'round? Remember the amazing words spoken to you?

That was a powerful night, one of the best of my life. I remember standing around the fire as the guys took turns sharing memories and validating me. Some said they believed in me, valued me deeply as a friend, and one even said he would follow me. I couldn't have asked for more.

As men, we always wonder if we are up for the next challenge, the next phase of our lives. "But can I handle *this*?" seems like the haunting question of masculinity, always staring us down. It's not the lions we've killed that capture our attention; it's the ones we know are waiting out there for us in the tall grass. So let me ask—right now, in this moment, at this juncture, where do you feel least sure about yourself?

I wish this wasn't the case, but I feel least sure in my ability to create a world for myself. What I mean is, *actually* finding a solid group of guys to walk life with, not just correspond with every so often, and *actually* finding or creating meaningful work, and actively creating a home and world with Susie. Part of the doubt comes from the past couple of years where work was really hard to find in general, let alone something I found to have meaning, and keeping or finding great guys was even more difficult. I know it is unfair to Susie, but I am afraid that in lieu of creating a world for myself I will eventually just hitch my wagon to her and let the world that she creates suffice for the one that I wasn't able to.

Then this is the next step you must take; this is the lion you must now slay.

I confess I hate this about the masculine journey, but it's true: just when you think you've arrived, you are called up again. As soon as we've begun to get a feel for the stage we are at, the next one comes knocking at the door. And though one stage really does prepare us for another, they are never quite the same and so once again we wonder if we have what it takes. It helps to repeat to yourself, *This isn't just me; this is the nature of the quest.*

But here's the thing: in some areas I still feel young. I mean, I am twenty-five years old, engaging in many arenas that are for men, but sometimes I still hear the voice of the boy in me.

Yes, I'm surprised how much I still do myself. It's embarrassing how often it happens, really. There was once a wholeheartedness that was ours, back in our original life in Eden, which our souls somehow remembers. But because of the war, because of a thousand different moments of disappointment, shame, or heartbreak, we are not wholehearted. There are young places within us still, there is a boy within, and it is the boy who often feels overwhelmed by the new mountain in front of us. I still remember how I felt on my wedding day (I was twenty-three just like you). There I was, a boy in a tuxedo, sitting in the pastor's office before the ceremony just . . . waiting. Through the door I heard the piano begin to play, and I knew I was about to burn my ships like Cortez, except they felt like toy boats and man did I feel young, way too young to be getting married. Was I making a colossal mistake?

I felt something from the same region of my chest going in for my first "real" job interview and though I put on a tie and borrowed a pair of dress shoes, I felt like they'd know immediately that I was faking it, pretending to be a man. It happened with promotions too—could I handle *this*? Then there was the day we said good-bye to family and boarded a plane for Washington DC; you were three months old, and we might just as well have been headed off across the prairie in a covered wagon never to see home or kin again; at least that's how I felt.

Those feelings can be really confusing. They make us doubt our decisions, feel like we are in way over our heads when in fact it is simply the boy inside freaking out because he feels that he has to handle our lives for us. Listen carefully—he does not. Every man is part boy and part man. God requires the man to step up and play the man; but to the boy he offers comfort and healing. Be kind to the boy inside. It is the man God is calling to face down the next lion, but the boy he treats with genuine kindness. Do the same—be kind to yourself, your fears, your feelings of inadequacy. Don't despise the fact that places in you still feel young; shame never heals, never encourages, never makes whole. Give grace to those places that feel six or ten or even thirteen.

That sounds really encouraging. So if it is the man in me, and not the little boy, that must face the coming lions, I think he is already cluing in to what's on the horizon. As I look forward into this next season, I am very aware that I have some weighty choices to make. For starters: Will I isolate? The cliché "no man is an island" jumps into my head and I want to gag. Instead I know I have already felt the pull to become more removed over the course of this decade and the next. Work begins to demand our time, and afterward I'm usually exhausted. Throw in Susie, and I am tempted to let her be all the relational connection I need. Connecting with guys feels really hard in the age of mass communication and social media. I still don't do very well on the phone . . . it's too abstract.

When I lived in California, hanging with guy friends meant drinking together. Almost exclusively. It was fun, and has its place, but if that is all there is to do, it doesn't feel very substantial. Now, when I *did something* with friends, whether it was running or sailing or working on the ranch or writing together, the connection felt much stronger. A few of my friends still on the West Coast will garden together, and I've been rock climbing with friends during these few months in Colorado. What I have learned is that we need to be doing something—collecting empty bottles doesn't count. It is really hard to cultivate this, and I can already feel the pull to not "waste my time" trying to make it happen, but I know that when I don't have good guys in my life I don't do well. I know I am not unique in my desire for close male friends, but it is first a choice to acknowledge it, and then a challenge, to seek it out. I read that book you talked about, *Shop Class as Soulcraft*, and at one point Crawford challenged the man who tries to be alone:

> The idea of autonomy denies that we are born into a world that existed prior to us. It posits an essential aloneness; an autonomous being is free in the sense that a being severed from all other beings is free. To regard oneself this way is to betray the natural debts we owe to the world, and commit the moral error of ingratitude. For in fact we are basically dependent beings: one upon another, and each on a world that is not of our making.[1]

After you brought this up the other day, I was thinking back on the guys who were my friends during my twenties, sifting through the memories to see if anything helpful stands out. Glen was a landscaping guy who was a few years older than me; we shared a love of rock climbing and British pubs. Brian befriended me when I first arrived at church, even though he had a career in sales and I was just finishing college; we made a point of going out for Mexican food once a week. As I moved into the corporate world, Jason became a close friend; we traveled a lot on the job, and there's nothing like a buddy you can gripe about work with at the end of the day. Frank and John were maybe my closest friends; we met in the theater company, and having that shared mission gave us a context for the camaraderie that grew between us.

None of them looked like the perfect fit. We were different ages; we came from different backgrounds; we were all really different personalities. Friends are like used cars, really—a little funky, not what you would have planned on, but you grow to love them. Be open to who God brings along; don't look too close at the upholstery. I also notice that all my friendships shared some sort of context or mission—climbing, work, the theater. You are so right about this. It's really huge for guys—you've got to have something to do bigger than drinking. It's in the context of doing stuff that the friendship solidifies.

I also realize with a bit of sadness that none of those guys stayed in my life past my twenties. I guess that's just how it goes—friendships have a season. I moved to DC; things changed, and that's okay. I only had one friend from high school that carried on into my twenties—Kyle—but he was more of an act of kindness than a peer, a guy I had a heart for and sort of threw a line to. It'll be important that you distinguish the two. God may call you to love and pour into some lost soul, but guys who drain you are not the same as good friends. Oh, and by the way—the boyfriends or husbands of Susie's friends probably aren't going to be the guys you want to hang out with one-on-one. Every wife wants it to work out that way, but it rarely does.

It is going to take some intentionality making friends in Minneapolis—especially since you always have it in the back of your mind that you guys probably won't stay beyond Susie's grad school. Volunteer with Habitat for Humanity; join the local running club; build trails with REI; join a small group at church. Good guys are out there, but you will have to make that choice to find them.

The culture of young men feels like Peter Pan's Neverland. Every choice to step up and play the man is opposed by the pull to take the path of least resistance, to not grow up. The boy in me wants to coast, to take the easier road, to play all the time. Deeper still, the boy in me is really good at thinking about myself, and for him fear is the great wolf stopping any action that might be difficult. All play and no work makes Jack . . . seriously undeveloped and useless. The boy suffers action, while the man takes action. When I sold my VW, I needed a bit more money to buy a nicer car, so I sold my motorcycle as well. I knew there wasn't much use for it in Minnesota, but more than that I knew it was a sacrifice that needed making in order to secure a better vehicle for the time being. I did not, however, sell my helmet. I know that motorcycles are in my future. I was not giving up on wildness; I was choosing to play the man and take action.

Toward the end of *The Alchemist*, Santiago is robbed again and beaten while digging for his treasure. Despite all that he has been through, he despairs at first:

"What are you doing here?" one of the figures demanded. Because he was terrified, the boy didn't answer. He had found where his treasure was, and was frightened at what might happen.[2]

The boy in him pouts and wallows in his predicament, until the man in him steps up to interpret the situation. The man in Santiago sees hardship as part of his journey, and by putting it in a context he is not broken by it, but sees the guiding role even his antagonists can take.

And they disappeared. The boy stood up shakily, and looked once more at the Pyramids. They seemed to laugh at him, and he laughed back, his heart bursting with joy.[3]

It feels like so much depends on how we interpret things, especially hardship. Every great story and strong hero that I admire is fraught with difficulty and setback, but they see it as training and opportunities to grow stronger. When hard times or difficult situations come, I, like Santiago, initially react as the boy, getting irritated and despairing at my poor situation. It is a choice to interpret as a man, seeing the context in my own story and choosing to take action, rather than suffer it.

I want a sense of mastery. In reading *Shop Class* I have been struck over and over at the need to feel competent in our world, to be the "master of our own things," as Crawford calls it. Again, the boy gets in here and fakes competency. A friend of mine (who will remain unnamed) worked for an online certification course company (which will also remain unnamed). This company offered courses in a variety of things: from installing drywall to handling black mold to basic electrician certification. My friend was a writer for these courses, and as such became an "expert" by researching the subject online, for about ten to thirty minutes, and would then write the course. For real. This is a fantastic example of faking competency; someone who never touched a conduit or carried drywall could bestow certification on someone else, for the right price.

Being willing to seek mastery of something, putting in the hours of work dealing with setbacks and the slow learning process, is extremely humbling and empowering. To hold true mastery over anything, be it sailing or building model ships or carpentry or bow hunting or Japanese, it instills the kind of general attitude of competency that sets apart the boy and the man. I can't help but wonder: Will I submit to the process? Will I hang in there?

Crawford has a series of mentors in his journey of motorcycle mechanics, one he calls Fred. Fred is a true master of old bikes, and Crawford takes time to be an apprentice in Fred's shop, learning things that can only be passed down through hands-on training. We all want that, in some capacity, I think. Having a guru or father we can learn from, to guide us down the path of mastery, may be the only way to really know we are heading in the right direction.

Now you are naming a truly deep longing in men. Blaine just commented to me the other day that every young guy he knows wishes that some older man would come along and say, "I've got a revolution; we need you; follow me." So I'd like to suggest that the single most important decision you will make in the coming years, the one that will have by far the biggest long-term impact, is this one: *Will I remain open to fathering?*

I don't mean from me, though I will always be here for you. I mean from your truest Father, your God.

Ethan is a young man in our community who I've been trying to help over the past couple of years. He doesn't have a father he can talk to like you and I have been doing; well, actually, he has had three dads but none of them offers him anything. He's learned to just go at life himself, and he's made a lot of painfully bad decisions. But he won't ask for help. He'll accept it—kind of—if I step in, but otherwise he just sort of throws himself at life like those carnival bumper cars, careening around, bouncing off stuff, but without the bumpers and with a lot more consequence.

There is an independent spirit that comes with the twenties, and in many ways it is right on time. You need to head off into your own life, make your own decisions, and assert your own mastery over your world. But thanks to the divorce generation and the adolescent culture, most young men seize that independent spirit like a banner and never look for any form of fathering. A host of Peter Pans. But as you have discovered, the thrill of self-determination soon gives way to loneliness and disorientation. We were never made to do life without a father; fatherhood is literally at the center of our universe. I know isolation has become our normal and it feels like freedom, but the trade-off just isn't worth it.

Whatever else we've tried to offer in the pages of this book, the backdrop of it all is what it might look like to receive fathering. This is the ache of every man's heart, whether he is conscious of it or not. Thomas Wolfe said, "The deepest search in life, it seemed to me, the thing that in one way or another was central to all living was man's search to find a father, not merely the lost father of his youth, but the image of a strength and wisdom external to his need and superior to his hunger, to which the belief and power of his own life could be united."[4]

Above and beyond a woman, a job, even our dreams, this is what we need—all of us.

That's not what it feels like at first. What we want right off the bat is a map of some kind, a plan, a clear path to begin walking down. Something that makes it clear what is important for us to do, and how to start doing it right now.

Right, and God doesn't give one. Nobody gets the master plan, not even a five-year overview—have you ever wondered why? The reason is simple and massively disruptive: God wants us to seek him, draw near to him, learn to walk with him, and frankly we won't do it if we have a plan to follow instead. I said in chapter two that man has an allergy to seeking God; it is sad but profoundly true. God laments in Jeremiah, "I thought you would call me 'Father,'" but they wouldn't (3:19).

You have a friend who is trying to figure out if and where to pursue a PhD, a friend who is trying to start a music career, another starting his own business, a fourth who has gotten married but doesn't know what to do next—are any of them asking God to father them? Are they seeking out the counsel of older men? You begin to see what I mean. I love the go-for-it zeal of young manhood, but too often it comes with a generous dose of I-don't-need-help-with-this and no fathering ever takes place. Not until they are thirty-eight or fifty-five and find themselves in a counselor's office with a collapsing marriage, runaway daughter, depression, anxiety, or a gambling addiction.

Our allergy to God is never more obvious than when we look at how few men seek him out as Father. I became a follower of Jesus at nineteen and knew God was our Father, but I lament that I have only sought his fathering in the past several years. (What *is* it with men—must we be so stubborn?) As George MacDonald said, "The hardest, gladdest thing in the world is to cry '*Father*!' from a full heart."[5] This from a man who had a really remarkable dad. Yes, it is awkward and unfamiliar territory for most of us. But the rewards of being fathered have no equal on earth.

Look at it this way: we need *guidance.* Is it time to buy or keep paying rent? Is the mechanic screwing me or should it cost $950 to repair a CV joint? How long does grief last? How do I help my child with night fears? We need *interpretation.* Is this merely a soul-killing job or is it my current lion? My girl is crying a lot—is this just a phase or something serious? Is my ache for a motorcycle and the open road the cry for a new life or do I just need a vacation? We need *encouragement* and *validation.* "You're doing great, this is right where you need to be; you can handle this next move, I know you can; I'm very proud of you." In other words, we need fathering—it is the deepest, most desperate need of our existence. Without it all you have left are your hunches, the sibling society, and the Internet. Adolescent boys cannot father adolescent boys. Think *Lord of the Flies.*

It begins with a posture—*I need a father; I have a father; I am going to seek my father.* Isn't that the turning point in the story of the prodigal son? He shook off his independence and took on a new posture, a willingness to turn father-ward . . . and it saved him.

This was the turning point in Santiago's story; come to think of it, this was core to every turning point in his story. First he has the encounter with Melchizedek who sets him on his adventure, but in typical twentysomething arrogance Santiago was irritated by the appearance of the old man on the bench next to him and simply wanted him to go away. Had he shooed the intruder off, he never would have gotten started. Once in Tangier he gets himself in trouble when he follows the young thief (the adolescent culture), but he is rescued when he turns to the old shopkeeper for help. Sometime later Santiago thinks he has found his life's meaning when he meets the beautiful young girl at the oasis, but it is the old alchemist himself who befriends him and sets him back on his quest. Maybe the reason we love the story is because it reverberates with father.

Ask God to father you, every day. I'm serious. As you wake in the morning, as you drive to work, as you face the new thing, say, "Father, I need you to help me today; I ask you to father me." Begin a practice of asking for it; then remember to ask for it when you realize you haven't asked in some time.

Next, keep an eye out for the many different ways it will come. God might bring a Fred along, a mentor for a particular need. The first year of our marriage we got into a nasty conflict with our land-lords; I didn't know what to do. God provided an attorney from our church to coach me through it. It took initiative on my part to seek him out, but he was wise and kind, and he saved me a lot of money and grief. Once the need was gone, he disappeared, like Melchizedek. For years Mom and I both drove old Volkswagens; God provided Tim, a master mechanic who loved talk radio, and I got hours under the hood with my own Fred. Our first pastor coached me through a terrible crisis of faith; the associate pastor taught me how to study the Bible. Just like there are friends for a season, God will provide a "father" for a season.

And how we need them.

My father died two years ago, on Father's Day weekend; it felt like an in-your-face, ironic dig. But he died in his heart many years before that. I am fifty-three and I still have so many questions; life keeps changing on me, too, asking more and more of me. I still need a father. And the day will come, Sam, when you'll be in the same position. What then? The grand design from before the world began was for every man to have a Father all the days of his life. This is available. As I have learned to walk with God and recognize his voice, he has rescued me over and over with his love, his counsel, and his playful encouragement. This is something to be practiced—just like you learned to ride a motorcycle or lead a 5.10.

I believe you young men are the warrior generation this world needs. I believe you will see very trying times, perhaps even the end of the age. The timing of *Halo*, the film adaptations of *The Lord of the Rings*, the resurgence of superheroes in film, and all the games and movies like these is curious indeed. Their epic, urgent, heroic battle cries were spoken at this moment in history—your moment. Perhaps it was orchestrated by an unseen hand. You have the strength and the courage to handle what is before you. You do. But you must not try to play Switzerland in this savage war; there is no neutral ground. The only safe move is to boldly take sides with the kingdom of God, take your position in the line. Make the decision to be fully in—to become the warrior, live in the larger story—and everything else will fall into place. "All things shall be added unto you." Really.

As I think back on my years as a young man, the words I longed to hear were the very words I still eagerly listen for today:

You're going to be okay.
You're going to find your way.
You are not alone.

That's really, really good. It's exactly what I need to hear. Maybe I'll tape those words to my bathroom mirror, because they are true, they are our birthright as sons of the Living One. "I'm going to be okay. I'm going to find my way. I am not alone."

What next? Where do I go from here?

It is our hope that after reading the book and completing the journal each of you will feel more equipped to face the world. (Yes—there is a *Killing Lions Journal*!) But the journey doesn't end here. We have created an online magazine in the ethos of inviting active community as we continue to explore what genuine masculinity looks like. It's called And Sons magazine. Come check us out: www.andsonsmagazine.com.

We have also created some killer adventure videos for you! They're free, so check them out: www.KillingLions.com.

We are doing live events for men. Come and join us! Check out "events" at www.ransomedheart.com.

Finally, cheers to you for taking the step to journey into this wilderness with us. It may not always be an easy road, but the fruits are worth it. Way to go! We're proud of you!

The Daily Prayer

My dear Lord Jesus, I come to you now to be restored in you, renewed in you, to receive your life and your love, and all the grace and mercy I so desperately need this day. I honor you as my Lord, and I surrender every aspect and dimension of my life to you. I give you my spirit, soul, and body; my heart, mind, and will. I cover myself with your blood—my spirit, soul, and body; my heart, mind, and will. I ask your Holy Spirit to restore me in you, renew me in you, and lead this time of prayer. In all that I now pray, I stand in total agreement with your Spirit, and with all those praying for me by the Spirit of God.

Dearest God, holy and victorious Trinity, you alone are worthy of all my worship, my heart's devotion, all my praise, all my trust, and all the glory of my life. I love you; I worship you; I give myself over to you in my heart's search for life. You alone are Life, and you have become my life. I renounce all other gods, every idol, and I give to you, God, the place in my heart and in my life that you truly deserve. This is all about you, and not about me. You are the Hero of this story, and I belong to you. I ask your forgiveness for my every sin. Search me, know me, and reveal to me where you are working in my life, and grant to me the grace of your healing, and deliverance, and a deep and true repentance.

Heavenly Father, thank you for loving me and choosing me before you made the world. You are my true Father—my creator, redeemer, sustainer, and the true end of all things, including my life. I love you; I trust you; I worship you. I give myself over to you, Father, to be one with you as Jesus is one with you. Thank you for proving your love for me by sending Jesus. I receive him and all his life and all his work, which you ordained for me. Thank you for including me in Christ, forgiving me my sins, granting me his righteousness, making me complete in him. Thank you for making me alive with Christ, raising me with him, seating me with him at your right hand, establishing me in his authority, and anointing me with your love and your Spirit and your favor. I receive it all with thanks and give it total claim to my life—my spirit, soul, and body; my heart, mind, and will.

Jesus, thank you for coming to ransom me with your own life. I love you, worship you, trust you. I give myself over to you, to be one with you in all things. I receive all the work and triumph of your cross, death, blood, and sacrifice for me, through which my every sin is atoned for. I am ransomed, delivered from the kingdom of darkness and transferred to your kingdom, my sin nature is removed, my heart circumcised unto God, and every claim being made against me is cancelled and disarmed. I take my place now in your cross and death, dying with you to sin, to my flesh, to this world, to the evil one and his kingdom. I take up the cross and crucify my flesh with all its pride, arrogance, unbelief, and idolatry [and anything else you are currently struggling with]. I put off the old man. Apply to me all the work and triumph in your cross, death, blood, and sacrifice. I receive it with thanks and give it total claim to my spirit, soul, and body; my heart, mind, and will.

Jesus, I also receive you as my Life, and I receive all the work and triumph in your resurrection, through which you have conquered sin, death, judgment, and the evil one. Death has no power over you, nor does any foul thing. And I have been raised with you to a new life, to live your life—dead to sin and alive to God. I take my place now in your resurrection and in your life, and I give my life to you to live your life. I am saved by your life. I reign in life through your life. I receive your hope, love, faith, joy; your goodness, trueness, wisdom, power, and strength. Apply to me all the work and triumph in your resurrection; I receive it with thanks, and I give it total claim to my spirit, soul, and body; my heart, mind, and will.

Jesus, I also sincerely receive you as my authority, rule, and dominion; my everlasting victory against Satan and his kingdom; and my ability to bring your kingdom at all times and in every way. I receive all the work and triumph in your ascension, through which Satan has been judged and cast down, all authority in heaven and on earth has been given to you. All authority in the heavens and on this earth has been given to you, Jesus, and you are worthy to receive all glory and honor, power and dominion, now and forever. I take my place now in your authority and in your throne, through which I have been raised with you to the right hand of the Father and established in your authority. I give myself to you, to reign with you always. Apply to me all the work and triumph in your authority and your throne; I receive it with thanks, and I give it total claim to my spirit, soul, and body; my heart, mind, and will.

I now bring the authority, rule, and dominion of the Lord Jesus Christ, and the full work of Christ, over my life today; over my home, my household, my work, over all my kingdom and domain. I bring the authority of the Lord Jesus Christ and the full work of Christ against every evil power coming against me—against every foul spirit, every foul power and device. [You might need to name them—what has been attacking you?] I cut them off in the name of the Lord; I bind and banish them from me and from my kingdom now, in the mighty name of Jesus Christ. I also bring the full work of Christ between me and every person, and I allow only the love of God and only the Spirit of God between us.

Holy Spirit, thank you for coming. I love you; I worship you; I trust you. I receive all the work and triumph in Pentecost, through which you have come, you have clothed me with power from on high, sealed me in Christ, become my union with the Father and the Son, the Spirit of truth in me, the life of God in me, my counselor, comforter, strength, and guide. I honor you as Lord, and I fully give to you every aspect and dimension of my spirit, soul, and body; my heart, mind, and will—to be filled with you, to walk in step with you in all things. Fill me afresh, Holy Spirit. Restore my union with the Father and the Son. Lead me into all truth, anoint me for all of my life and walk and calling, and lead me deeper into Jesus today. I receive you with thanks, and I give you total claim to my life.

Heavenly Father, thank you for granting to me every spiritual blessing in Christ Jesus. I claim the riches in Christ Jesus over my life today. I bring the blood of Christ once more over my spirit, soul, and body; over my heart, mind, and will. I put on the full armor of God—the belt of truth, breastplate of righteousness, shoes of the gospel, helmet of salvation; I take up the shield of faith and sword of the Spirit, and I choose to be strong in the Lord and in the strength of your might, to pray at all times in the Spirit.

Jesus, thank you for your angels. I summon them in the name of Jesus Christ and instruct them to destroy all that is raised against me, to establish your kingdom over me, to guard me day and night. I ask you to send forth your Spirit to raise up prayer and intercession for me. I now call forth the kingdom of God throughout my home, my household, my kingdom and domain in the authority of the Lord Jesus Christ, giving all glory and honor and thanks to him. In Jesus' name, amen.

A Prayer for Guidance

A few thoughts in seeking guidance from God . . .

First, do whatever you can to release the pressure. Pressure always gets in the way of us hearing from God. You'll find it helpful to lay down the pressure as you seek for guidance. Drama never helps; stress never helps. Take a deep breath. Give this some space.

Second, be open to whatever God has to say to you. If you are in fact really only open to hearing one answer from God ("yes"), then it's not likely you will hear anything at all. Or if you do hear what you hope to hear, you'll have a hard time trusting it was God speaking. The key is surrender—yielding your desires and plans and hunches to the Living God, so that you might receive from him something far better: his counsel.

Finally, give it some time. Pray this prayer for several days, or even better, several weeks when it comes to major decisions; give God room to speak to you. For he *does* speak, and it is your right as his son to hear his voice:

> He wakens me morning by morning,
>> wakens my ear to listen like one being taught. (Isa. 50:4)

He calls his own sheep by name and leads them out . . . he goes on ahead of them, and his sheep follow him because they know his voice. (John 10:3–4)

God speaks. We hear. That is part of the basic Christian life.

Father, I come to you in need of your counsel, your guidance and direction. But first I lay my life before you; I consecrate my entire life to you, including all my plans and decisions. I give all of my hopes and dreams, all my desires, and all my fears to you, God. I surrender my hunches, my own thoughts and plans, and I ask you, God, for your clear and true leading in my life. You have promised me, "I will instruct you and teach you in the way you should go; I will counsel you and watch over you" (Ps. 32:8). I need your counsel, God. Come into this decision-making process. Shine your light here and banish all confusion; deliver me from falsehood and fear, from false directions and foolish choices. I want to know the way you have for me. I also lay down in this moment the pressure to get the answer right; I lay down the pressure to hear from you clearly. I simply ask you to speak to me, God, to guide me as a Father.

At this point get specific—"Do you want me to take this job?" or, "Do you want me to date this girl?" Pause, and listen. If you think you are hearing from God, ask him to confirm it. Confirmation is *really* important when it comes to big decisions like moving overseas or who you are going to marry.

Father, thank you for speaking to me on this. Now I ask you to confirm your counsel through another source. Speak to me through your Word, or the counsel of others. Bring me confirmation, Lord.

If you haven't heard anything yet, try another round of prayer:

Father, I need your counsel, your guidance and direction. I lay my life before you now; I consecrate my entire life completely to you. You promised me that you would instruct me and teach me in the way I should go. I need your counsel, God. Come into this decision-making process. Shine your light here and banish all confusion; deliver me from falsehood and fear, from false directions and foolish choices. I want to know the way you have for me. I lay down the pressure to get the answer right; I lay down the pressure to hear from you clearly. I simply ask you to speak to me, God, to guide me as a Father. Do you want me to [ask a specific question]? Is this your will for me?

We've found it helpful to linger with the question, listening to God while we repeat the question:

Father, do you want me to [ask a specific question]? Is this your will for me?

We've also found it helpful to "try on" an answer and see if the Lord confirms it:

Are you saying yes, Father—you want me to [fill in the question]? Or are you saying no, this is not what you want for me?

Pause, and listen. If you still aren't getting clarity, walk away and let it rest for a while. Take up the prayer again later, or tomorrow. God will speak.

If for some reason you have to make a decision now (Do you *really* have to make the decision now? This can't wait one more day?), then use your best judgment but add this prayer:

> Father, I ask you to come into this decision; I pray you would block my path if I haven't chosen well. Close every door, thwart every move if this isn't your will for me. Come and guide me.

> God *will* guide you, friends. He loves you like a son.

A Prayer for Sexual Healing

Healing for your sexuality is available; this is a very hopeful truth! But you must realize that your sexuality is deep and core to your nature as a human being. Therefore sexual brokenness can be one of the deepest types of brokenness a person might experience. You must take your healing and restoration seriously. This guided prayer will help immensely. You may find you need to pray through it a few times in order to experience a lasting freedom.

A bit of explanation on the reasons for the prayer: First, when we misuse our sexuality through sin, we give Satan an open door to oppress us in our sexuality. A man who uses pornography will find himself in a very deep struggle with lust; a woman who was sexually promiscuous before marriage may find herself wresting with sexual temptation years afterward. So it is important to bring our sexuality under the lordship (and therefore protection) of the Lord Jesus Christ and seek his cleansing of our sexual sins.

Second, sexual brokenness—whether through abuse of our sexuality by our own actions or by the actions of others—can create sexual difficulties, and also opens the door for the enemy to oppress us. Quite often forgiveness is needed—both the confidence that we are forgiven by the Lord and the choice we make to forgive others. This will prove immensely freeing.

Let us begin by bringing our lives and sexuality under the lordship of Jesus Christ:

> Lord Jesus Christ, I confess here and now that you are my Creator (John 1:3) and therefore the creator of my sexuality. I confess that you are also my Savior, that you have ransomed me with your blood (Matt. 20:28; 1 Cor. 15:3). I have been bought with the blood of Jesus Christ; my life and my body belong to God (1 Cor. 6:19–20). Jesus, I present myself to you now to be made whole and holy in every way, including in my sexuality. You ask us to present our bodies to you as living sacrifices (Rom. 12:1) and the parts of our bodies as instruments of righteousness (Rom. 6:13). I do this now. I present my body, my sexuality ["as a man" or "as a woman"], and I present my sexual nature to you. I consecrate my sexuality to Jesus Christ.

Next you need to renounce the ways you have misused your sexuality. The more specific you can be, the more helpful this will be. God created your sexuality for pleasure and joy within the context of the marriage covenant. Sexual activity outside of marriage can be very damaging to a person and to their relationships (1 Cor. 6:18–20). What you want to do in this part of the prayer is confess and renounce all sexual sin—for example, sexual intimacy outside of marriage; not only intercourse but other forms of sexual intimacy, such as mutual masturbation or oral sex. Many people assume these "don't really count as sin" because they didn't result in actual intercourse; however, there was sexual stimulation and intimacy outside marriage. Keep in mind there is the "spirit of the law" and the "letter of the law." What matters are issues of heart and mind as well as body. Other examples of sins to renounce would be extramarital affairs, the use of pornography, and sexual fantasies. You may know exactly what you need to confess and renounce; you may need to ask God's help to remember. Take your time here. As memories and events come to mind, confess and renounce them. For example: "Lord Jesus, I ask your forgiveness for my sins of masturbation and using pornography. I renounce those sins in your name." After you have confessed your sins, go on with the rest of the prayer.

> Jesus, I ask your Holy Spirit to help me now remember, confess, and renounce my sexual sins. [Pause. Listen. Remember. Confess and renounce.] Lord Jesus, I ask your forgiveness for every act of sexual sin. You promised that if we confess our sins you are faithful and just to forgive us our sins and cleanse us from all unrighteousness (1 John 1:9). I ask you to cleanse me of my sexual sins now; cleanse my body, soul, and spirit; cleanse my heart and mind and will; cleanse my sexuality. Thank you for forgiving me and cleansing me. I receive your forgiveness and cleansing. I renounce every claim I have given Satan to my life or sexuality through my sexual sins. Those claims are now broken by the cross and blood of Jesus Christ (Col. 2:13–15).

Next comes forgiveness. It is vital that you forgive both yourself and those who have harmed you sexually. Listen carefully: Forgiveness is a choice; we often have to make the decision to forgive long before we feel forgiving. We realize this can be difficult, but the freedom you will find will be worth it! Forgiveness is not saying, "It didn't hurt me." Forgiveness is not saying, "It didn't matter." Forgiveness is the act whereby we pardon the person, we release them from all bitterness and judgment. We give them to God to deal with.

Lord Jesus, I thank you for offering me total and complete forgiveness. I receive that forgiveness now. I choose to forgive myself for all of my sexual wrongdoing. I also choose to forgive those who have harmed me sexually. [Be specific here; name those people and forgive them.] I release them to you. I release all my anger and judgment toward them. Come, Lord Jesus, into the pain they caused me, and heal me with your love.

This next step involves breaking the unhealthy emotional and spiritual bonds formed with other people through sexual sin. One of the reasons the Bible takes sexual sin so seriously is because of the damage it does. Another reason is because of the bonds it forms with people, bonds meant to be formed only between husband and wife (1 Cor. 6:15–20). One of the marvelous effects of the cross of our Lord Jesus Christ is that it breaks these unhealthy bonds. "May I never boast except in the cross of our Lord Jesus Christ, through which the world has been crucified to me, and I to the world" (Gal. 6:14).

I now bring the cross of my Lord Jesus Christ between me and every person with whom I have been sexually intimate. [Name them specifically whenever possible. Also, name those who have abused you sexually.] I break all sexual, emotional, and spiritual bonds with [name if possible, or just "that girl in high school" if you can't remember her name]. I keep the cross of Christ between us.

Many people experience negative consequences through the misuse of their sexuality. Those consequences might be lingering guilt (even after confession) or repeated sexual temptation. Consequences might also be the inability to enjoy sex with their spouses. It will help to bring the work of Christ here as well. Many people end up making unhealthy "agreements" about sex or themselves, about men or women or intimacy, because of the damage they have experienced through sexual sin (their sins, or the sin of someone against them). You will want to ask Christ what those agreements are, and break them!

Lord Jesus, I ask you to reveal to me every "agreement" I have made about my sexuality or this specific struggle. [An example would be "I will always struggle with this" or "I can never get free" or "I don't deserve to enjoy sex now" or "My sexuality is dirty." Pause and let Jesus reveal those agreements to you. Then break them.] I break this agreement [name it] in the name of my Lord Jesus Christ, and I renounce every claim I have given it in my life. I renounce [name what the struggle is—"the inability to have an orgasm" or "this lingering shame" or "the hatred of my body"]. I bring the cross and blood of Jesus Christ against this [guilt or shame, every negative consequence]. I banish my enemy from my sexuality in the mighty name of the Lord Jesus Christ. I invite the healing presence of Jesus Christ to cleanse me, and restore me as a sexual being in fullness of joy and wholeness. I ask you, Jesus, to fill my sexuality with your holiness, to strengthen me and restore me in your name.

Finally, it will prove helpful to consecrate your sexuality to Jesus Christ once more.

Lord Jesus, I now consecrate my sexuality to you in every way. I consecrate my sexual intimacy with my spouse to you. I ask you to cleanse and heal my sexuality and our sexual intimacy in every way. I ask your healing grace to come and free me from all consequences of sexual sin. I ask you to fill my sexuality with your healing love and goodness. Restore my sexuality in wholeness. Let my spouse and me experience all of the intimacy and pleasure you intended a man and woman to enjoy in marriage. I invite the Spirit of God to fill our marriage bed. I pray all of this in the name of Jesus Christ my Lord. Amen!

We could report many stories of stunning redemption that have come as a result of individuals and couples praying through this type of prayer. Now remember—sometimes the wounds and consequences take time to heal. You might want to revisit this prayer several times over if lasting healing has not yet taken place. You may recall actions that need confession later; return to this prayer, and confess those as well. Some of you will also benefit from seeing a good Christian counselor. Hold fast to these truths:

- You, your body, and your sexuality belong to Jesus Christ.
- He has completely forgiven you.
- He created your sexuality to be whole and holy.
- He created your sexuality to be a source of intimacy and joy.
- Jesus Christ came to seek and save "what was lost" (Luke 19:10), including all that was lost in the blessings he intended through our sexuality.

Acknowledgments

With thanks to our agents Curtis and Sealy Yates, our editor Joel Miller, and to Brian Hampton and the team at Thomas Nelson.

About the Authors

John Eldredge is the author of numerous best-selling books including *Wild at Heart*, *Fathered by God*, and *Beautiful Outlaw*. He is also director of Ransomed Heart, a ministry devoted to restoring men and women in the love of God. John lives in Colorado but adventures around the world—often with his sons.

Sam Eldredge began his writing career in second grade with a memorable essay on penguins. He graduated with a bachelors in English and is currently working on an online magazine for men. When he goes out of doors he loves to drive motorcycles, sail, and adventure with his wife, Susie.

Notes

Chapter One

1. William Strauss and Neil Howe, *The Fourth Turning*, reprint edition (New York: Broadway Books, 1997).
2. Frederick Buechner, *Wishful Thinking: A Seeker's ABC* (San Francisco: HarperCollins, 1993), 95.
3. *Kingdom of Heaven*, directed by Ridley Scott, Twentieth Century Fox, 2005.
4. Fyodor Dostoevsky, *The Brothers Karamazov* (New York: Macmillan, 2002), eBook, 43.
5. Robert Bly, *The Sibling Society* (Boston: Addison-Wesley, 1996), vii.
6. Paulo Coelho, *The Alchemist*, English translation (New York: HarperCollins, 1998), 21.
7. Ibid., 18.
8. Ibid., 76.
9. Wallace Stevens, quoted in George S. Lensing, *Wallace Stevens: A Poet's Growth* (Baton Rouge: LSU Press 1991), 220.
10. "Grasslands: The Roots of Power," *Human Planet*, season 1, episode 6, directed by Tuppence Stone, aired February 17, 2011 (BBC America, 2011), DVD.

Chapter Two

1. Matt Lynley, "Here's How Much the Owners of Angry Birds Are Actually Worth," *Business Insider*, February 23, 2012, www.business insider.com/heres-how-much-the-owners-of-angry-birds-are-actually -worth-2012-2.

2. Walt Harrington, *The Everlasting Stream* (New York: Grove Press, 2002), 196–97.

3. G. K. Chesterton, *Orthodoxy* (New York: John Lane Company, 1908), 53.

Chapter Three

1. Coelho, *The Alchemist*, 92–93.

2. The Pew Research Center, "Marriage Rate Declines and Marriage Age Rises," December 14, 2011, http://www.pewsocialtrends.org /2011/12/14/marriage-rate-declines-and-marriage-age-rises/.

Chapter Four

1. John Watson, quoted in Sir William Robertson, *"Ian Maclaren": The Life of the Rev. John Watson, Part 4* (New York: Dodd, Mead 1908), 117.

2. Walker Percy, quoted in Os Guinness, *The Call: Finding and Fulfilling the Central Purpose of Your Life* (Nashville: Thomas Nelson 1993), 3.

3. *The Lord of the Rings: The Return of the King*, directed by Peter Jackson, New Line Cinema, 2003.

4. *Robin Hood*, directed by Ridley Scott, Universal Pictures, 2010.

5. Stephen Ambrose, *Comrades* (New York: Simon & Schuster, 1999), 61, 64–65.

Chapter Five

1. John Steinbeck, *The Log from the Sea of Cortez* (New York: Penguin Books, 1951), 14.

2. *As Good as It Gets*, directed by James Brooks, TriStar Pictures, 1997.

3. Dean Koontz, *Brother Odd* (New York: Random House, 2006), 87.

4. Mary Oliver, "The Summer Day," *House of Light* (Boston: Beacon Press, 2012).

5. *Jerry Maguire*, directed by Cameron Crowe, TriStar Pictures, 1996.

Chapter Six

1. Coelho, *The Alchemist*, 17.

2. Dr. Seuss, *Oh the Places You'll Go* (New York: Random House, 1960), 2.

3. Sheena Iyengar, quoted in Alina Tugend, "Too Many Choices: A Problem That Can Paralyze," February 26, 2010, http://www.nytimes.com/2010/02/27/your-money/27shortcuts.html?_r=0.

4. Viktor Frankl, *Man's Search for Meaning* (Boston: Beacon Press, 1992), 75.

5. Søren Kierkegaard, *Provocations* (Walden, NY: Plough Publishing, 1999), 4.

6. Lyle W. Dorsett, ed., *The Essential C. S. Lewis* (New York: Touchstone, 1988), 390.

Chapter Seven

1. David Barker and David Bearce, "End-Times Theology, the Shadow of the Future, and Public Resistance to Addressing Global Climate Change," *Political Science Quarterly*, June 2013, vol. 66, no. 2, 267–279, http://prq.sagepub.com/content/66/2/267.abstract?etoc.

2. VGChartz, "Halo: Combat Evolved," accessed February 20, 2014, http://www.vgchartz.com/game/939/halo-combat-evolved/.

3. *The Lord of the Rings: The Two Towers*, directed by Peter Jackson, New Line Cinema, 2002.

4. Joseph Campbell, *The Hero with a Thousand Faces* (New York: Pantheon Books, 1949).

Chapter Eight

1. Augustine, quoted in Garry Willis, *Saint Augustine: A Life* (New York: Penguin 1999), 2.

2. Allan Bloom, *Closing of the American Mind* (New York: Simon & Schuster, 1987), 26.

3. Karl Marx, *Marx on Religion* (Philadelphia: Temple University Press, 2002), 5.

4. Irvin D. Yalom, *Love's Executioner* (New York: HarperCollins, 1989), 6–7.

5. Anne Lamott, *Bird by Bird* (New York: Anchor Books, 1995), 22.

6. C. S. Lewis, *The Last Battle* (New York: HarperCollins, 1984), 189.

7. Dallas Willard, *The Divine Conspiracy* (New York: HarperCollins,

1998), xvi.

8. William Shakespeare, *Macbeth* (London: Macmillan and Co., 1893), 71.
9. Saint Athanasius, *Letter to Marcellinus* (Mahwah, NJ: Paulist Press, 1980), 101.
10. Saint Augustine of Hippo, *Saint Augustine's Confessions* (Mt. Juliet: Sovereign Grace Publications 2001), 1.
11. Chesterton, *Orthodoxy*, 185.

Chapter Nine

1. Kirk Woodward, "The Most Famous Thing Jean-Paul Sartre Never Said," *Rick on Theater*, July 9, 2010, http://rickontheater.blogspot.com/2010/07/most-famous-thing-jean-paul-sartre.html.

Chapter Ten

1. Matthew B. Crawford, *Shop Class as Soulcraft* (New York: Penguin Group, 2009), 208.
2. Coelho, *The Alchemist*, 91.
3. Ibid., 92.
4. C. Hugh Holman, ed., *The Thomas Wolfe Reader* (New York: Charles Scribner's Sons, 1962), 28.
5. Rolland Hein, ed., *The Heart of George MacDonald* (Vancouver: Regent College Publishing, 2004), 372.

MORE THAN A BOOK,

KILLING LIONS

IS AN INVITATION INTO A JOURNEY.

GO TO KILLINGLIONS.COM TO EXPERIENCE MORE.

9781400206704-A

Articles, photos and videos on Adventure, Beauty, God, Growing, The Woman, Good Things, and Engaging the World.

A free monthly online magazine for men.

YOUR SPACE TO CHASE DREAMS.

CAPTURE WISDOM.

CREATE A BATTLE PLAN.

EVEN KILL SOME LIONS.